Tuan Anh Vu

Essays On The Innovation And Intellectual Property System In Vietnam

Tuan Anh Vu

Essays On The Innovation And Intellectual Property System In Vietnam

LAP LAMBERT Academic Publishing

Impressum / Imprint

Bibliografische Information der Deutschen Nationalbibliothek: Die Deutsche Nationalbibliothek verzeichnet diese Publikation in der Deutschen Nationalbibliografie; detaillierte bibliografische Daten sind im Internet über http://dnb.d-nb.de abrufbar.

Alle in diesem Buch genannten Marken und Produktnamen unterliegen warenzeichen-, marken- oder patentrechtlichem Schutz bzw. sind Warenzeichen oder eingetragene Warenzeichen der jeweiligen Inhaber. Die Wiedergabe von Marken, Produktnamen, Gebrauchsnamen, Handelsnamen, Warenbezeichnungen u.s.w. in diesem Werk berechtigt auch ohne besondere Kennzeichnung nicht zu der Annahme, dass solche Namen im Sinne der Warenzeichen- und Markenschutzgesetzgebung als frei zu betrachten wären und daher von jedermann benutzt werden dürften.

Bibliographic information published by the Deutsche Nationalbibliothek: The Deutsche Nationalbibliothek lists this publication in the Deutsche Nationalbibliografie; detailed bibliographic data are available in the Internet at http://dnb.d-nb.de.

Any brand names and product names mentioned in this book are subject to trademark, brand or patent protection and are trademarks or registered trademarks of their respective holders. The use of brand names, product names, common names, trade names, product descriptions etc. even without a particular marking in this works is in no way to be construed to mean that such names may be regarded as unrestricted in respect of trademark and brand protection legislation and could thus be used by anyone.

Coverbild / Cover image: www.ingimage.com

Verlag / Publisher:
LAP LAMBERT Academic Publishing
ist ein Imprint der / is a trademark of
OmniScriptum GmbH & Co. KG
Heinrich-Böcking-Str. 6-8, 66121 Saarbrücken, Deutschland / Germany
Email: info@lap-publishing.com

Herstellung: siehe letzte Seite /
Printed at: see last page
ISBN: 978-3-659-55619-7

Zugl. / Approved by: Brussels, Solvay Brussels School of Economics and Management, Université Libre De Bruxelles, 2012

ACKNOWLEDGMENT

This dissertation would not be what it is now, if I was not received guidance, comments and supports from promoters, jury members of the defense, Belgian Technical Cooperation (BTC), my family, friends, colleagues and my employer, National Economics University-Vietnam (NEU).

Prior to the first meeting with Prof. Bruno Van Pottelsberghe de la Potterie at the end of 2004, I had neither knowledge nor interests on innovation and intellectual property. The meeting has totally changed my interests and shifted my research work to a different direction. With his inspiration and stimulation, I realized that innovation is critical to a sustainable growth of Vietnam's economy. I owed Prof. Bruno Van Pottelsberghe de la Potterie very much for his support, guidance, patience, challenge, stimulation, sympathy, and kindness. Probably, I would have never reached to this state of the research, if I have had another promoter. Moreover, taking this chance, I highly appreciate the jury members: Prof. Catherine Fallon, Prof. Anne Drumaux, Prof. Carine Peeters, and Prof. Michele Cincera for giving me such valuable comments and related articles for my research.

Although, it is not required by ULB, I also have a local promoter, Prof. Tran Tho Dat, to whom I owed an appreciation for his supports both in career and academic research. His advice and network has enabled me collect valuable data, information and judgments over my research work.

Taking this opportunity, I would like to thank my Belgian friend, Daniel Van Houtte. Daniel has been my close friend in both working place and social activities since 2003. Without Daniel's suggestions and recommendation, I might have never got in touch with respectful Prof. Jacques Nagels and Prof. Anne Drumaux for their initiative administrative supports.

Further, I highly appreciate the Belgian Technical Cooperation (BTC) for supporting me both in finance and administrative procedures, which allow me to follow this research work. Great thanks to Daphne, Nicolas, Françoise, Thanh Huong and other BTC's staff, who have provided essential supports and assistance when needed.

Additionally, I would like to send a great appreciation to my family: my parents, my wife and little daughter Minh Ngoc. They have always behind me with love, encouragement, stimulation and support to give me more strength to cross over challenges and difficulties.

EXECUTIVE SUMMARY

In the last two decades, Vietnam has gone through major changes in economic system and institutional system. These changes have sky-rocked the growth of non-SOE and attracted more foreign investments, while decreasing a considerable number of SOE through process of privatization or dissolve. In 2009, non-SOEs were accounted for over 96% of total firms and contributed about 46% to the GDP, while foreign firms and SOE were accounted about 2.4% and 1.6% of total firms, but respectively contributed 19% and 35% to GDP. Despite the fast growing in GDP, Vietnam has shown that its institution, science and technology and education are not supporting its development's state. Although, there has been an increasing in both number of patents filed and patent granted since the last two decades, the number of patents has been very small in comparison to many other developing countries in the region. This at least confirmed that Vietnam's science and technology is still primitive and therefore, policy makers should find ways to stimulate firms' innovation.

As, innovation is an economic indicator, and it has been widely measured by many researchers through the propensity to patent. Relying on the Oslo manual and the work of Peteers and van Pottelsberghe (2003), this research utilizes the form of questions and the structure of analysis to determine manufacturing firms' characteristics and their competencies, which might indicate firms' innovation. The two sources of data: the World Bank data and an in-depth interview with active technological firms have been used for analysis. Applying probit regression function with patent is the dependent variable on this set of data. The empirical outcomes suggest that the age and legal business types of the firm are the determinant characteristics of firms' innovation. Further analysis found that firm's innovation is also reflected through its innovation culture, such as: rewarding scheme; studying support; and involving with program CT168. Moreover, the empirical findings also acknowledge that supplier, customer, university personnel and patent document are critical external sources for innovative ideas. In addition to those competencies, personal competence has also found to be significant importance for firms' innovativeness.

Since, patent is used to analyze firms' innovation, taking this opportunity this research dives through the patenting system in developing ASEAN countries and China. This research found that FDIs positively correlated with the patent filings that imply that FDIs stimulate innovation. Furthermore, the relationship between patenting cost and demand for patent is followed a non linear traditional demand curve. Lower cost may stimulate more patents but increase workload for patent examiners, leading to the issue of patent quality. These findings suggest that patent cost can be used as a tool to stimulate patent filings.

Appropriability conditions have been perceived as weak in Vietnam. Administrative measure is the most common tool, which has been exercised in fighting for infringements. Taking 40 infringement cases, which have been recorded by NOIP and MOST, this research found that the values of fines are often much smaller than the actual infringed amounts. This reflects that the amount of fine is bounded by the maximum amount of fine (about 24,000 USD), which was ruled by the administrative execution ordinance. This explains that why most of infringement cases are handled by administrative measure. In addition to this study also found that administrative measure took much less time than court proceeding. The time required for court proceeding might take 10 or more times longer than the administrative procedure. This suggests that the regulation needs to be adjusted and administrative procedure in the judicial measure needs to be reformed.

Standing at the point of a policy maker, this research suggests that there should be one short term plan and one long term plan. In a short term, the government should provide more IP knowledge to people and firms through programs, such as CT168. Furthermore, working condition and infrastructure are essentially needed to be reformed for employees to generate new ideas. In addition to that, this dissertation also suggests a mechanism that allows industry and academic institution jointly collaborate for development of a new product or a new process. In a longer term plan, reformation on administrative measure, judicial measure and education are essential. Administrative measure should be limited to identifying problems, collecting evidences, and filing for a prosecution in criminal case. Further reformation to administrative procedure in judicial system is essential to allow people and firms easily access courts for trials. Furthermore, the maximum amount of fine should be ruled to about 2.5 times of real value of the goods, which are being infringed. In spite of the weaknesses of the education system and its importance for firms' innovation, a complete reformation in teaching curriculums is a must and it should create positive effects on all stake holders.

TABLE OF CONTENT

ABBREVIATION

APEC	Asia Pacific Economic Cooperation
ASEAN	Association of Southeast Asian Nations
DGIP	DGIP (Directorate General of Intellectual Property)
DIP	DIP (Department of Intellectual Property)
EPO	European Patent Office
FDI	Foreign Direct Investment
GSO	General Statistics Office of Vietnam
IMF	International Monetary Fund
IP	Intellectual Property
IPOP	IPOP (Intellectual Property Office of the Philippines)
IPOS	IPOS (Intellectual Property Office of Singapore)
IPR	Intellectual Property Rights
JPO	Japan Patent Office
MOET	Ministry of Education and Training
MOST	Ministry of Science and Technology
MyIPO	Intellectual Property Corporation of Malaysia (MyIPO)
NOIP	National Office of Intellectual Property
NPO	National Patent Office
OECD	Organisation for Economic Co-operation and Development
PPP	Purchasing Power Parity
SOE	State Owned Enterprise
UNCTAD	United Nations Conference on Trade and Development
USPTO	United States Patent and Trademark Office
USTR	Office of the United States Trade Representative
VCCI	Vietnam Chamber of Commerce and Industry
WEF	World Economics Forum
WIPO	World Intellectual Property Organization
WTO	World Trade Organization

TABLE OF FIGURES

TABLES

CHAPTER 1. INTRODUCTION

1.1 Purpose of the dissertation

Since Vietnam officially became a member of the WTO in 2007, topics relating to IP and IPRs have been even more promulgated widely in public media. A thirty minutes TV program, which provides basic intellectual property (IP) knowledge to people, has been broadcasted every Saturday's morning. Concurrently, many trainings, seminars and workshops have been organized in many cities and provinces of Vietnam under the project 168, which has been a key project of Ministry of Science and Technology, targeting both science researchers and companies. There has not been much statistical data to show the successfulness of this project. However, the dissemination of IP knowledge under this project surely catches the attention of local authorities and leverages the awareness of researchers and entrepreneurs. These positive outcomes are credited to the passion and hard working of IP staff at NOIP and local authorities for the past decade. So why intellectual property is important for economic growth and it has even been regulated in the TRIPS as a mandated requirement for the accession to the WTO. Well, an idea behind the IP is to ensure authors and inventors get adequate protection for their new or innovative products, which are the drivers for the growth of economy and changes in the society. Therefore, researches on innovation and intellectual property have been accumulated throughout decades. Well known economist, such as Schumpeter (1932) emphasized the important role of industrial innovation to the growth of economy. He is probably the pioneer, who put the first stone in building the castle of knowledge of innovation. Following that, the notion of innovation have been accumulated and the booming of researches on innovation and IP have been well noticed since the last decade of the 20 century and there has not been a sight of slowing down in the dawn of the 21 century.

Learning from the fact that, technological innovation has crucially contributed to the economics growth of countries in the Asian region, namely China, Indonesia, the Philippines, Singapore, Thailand and many other countries. Shamefully, the technological innovation in Vietnam has been constrained by many factors, including the weakness of institutional system, the disintegration to the world of science and technology and so on. Hence, one may ask what Vietnam would learn from countries in the region and from high tech country like US, French and Germany. Surely, the outcomes of the learning would stimulate or assist policy makers to create rules and regulation which help boosting innovative activities, which consequentially lead to innovative technologies. Industrialization is in the top of priority list of the strategic economics development of Vietnam, which has been consistently and clearly stated throughout many National assembly meetings since the "Doi Moi". Therefore, technological innovation plays an important role in the industrialization process. In another way, technological innovation is the driver for leveraging quantity and quality of products producing by manufactures, which in turn contribute to the economic growth. The purpose of this dissertation is to assist policies makers in making policies that stimulate innovative activities of manufacturing firms. In order to do so, this dissertation focuses on three issues: the manufacturing firm competencies; the patenting cost; the IPR enforcement. By studying these three issues in details, this dissertation hopes to provide policy makers with some crucial information for policy making process. However, before jumping to the hierarchical order of this dissertation, a brief summary of Vietnam's economy, science and technology, institutional systems over last two decades would serve as background information for judgment throughout this dissertation.

1.2 Economy, Institution, Education, and Science Technology of Vietnam in the period of 1990-2010.

1.2.1 Overall picture of Vietnamese economy

The economic reform in 1986 has enabled Vietnam lower poverty rate, created more businesses and attracted more foreign investments. World bank's data (2009) shows that the poverty rate (people earning less than $1.25 international dollar a day) was dropped impressively from 49,6% in 1998 to about 13% in 2008. GDP per capita at current US dollar was grown almost 8 times from $142 in 1991 to $1,172 in 2010. This impressive growth stemmed from the open policies on investment, trade and taking advantages of young and cheap labor cost.

Indeed Vietnam is still an agricultural base country with young population. As in 2009, about 69% of the population[1] was in the working age[2] and approximately 50% of the labor forces were working in agriculture businesses. However, the

---

[1] In accordance to Statistics Office of Vietnam, the population of Vietnam was approximately 87 millions (2009)
[2] Working age is between 15 and 64 (General Statistics Office of Vietnam)

economic outcome was inadequate in comparison to the intensity of the labor forces. As table 1.1 provides, in 2009 agriculture business generated only about 66 billion international dollar, which is accounted for only about 11% of the total incomes. In opposite, industrial business sector and service business sector utilized only 20% and 30% of the labor force respectively, but they contributed about 5 and 3 times more than the amount, which was contributed by agriculture business sector.

Table 1.1 Economic output generated by economic sectors

Sector	Agriculture		Industry		Service	
Unit	Trillion VND	Billion International Dollar	Trillion VND	Billion International Dollar	Trillion VND	Billion International Dollar
2006	197.9	40.4	1,199.1	244.9	480.3	98.1
2007	236.9	46.0	1,466.5	284.9	746.2	145.0
2008	377.2	61.3	1,903.1	309.3	1,007.2	163.7
2009	430.2	66.6	2,298.1	355.5	1,238.1	191.5

Source: Vietnam Statistical Year Book (2010) and IMF.

1.2.1.1 Agriculture

Agriculture has played an important role in the economics of Vietnam. Prior to the 1990s, the economy heavily relied on agriculture, with more than 70% of Vietnamese population participated in the agriculture business sectors. Despite the fact, in that period, Vietnam had been facing serious problems with food insecurity. The economy had relied very much on the support of the former Soviet Union and China. Undergone with the economic reform, in 1999 Vietnam was recognized as an important agricultural products' exporter in Asia. Applying innovative cultivation processes, agriculture business sectors has been able to raise their productivity with less labor force. As recorded in 2009, less than 50% of the labor forces were in agriculture business sector, but Vietnam was still ranked the 2nd country in Asia for rice production (GSO, 2011). Rice, tea, coffee, pepper, rubber, fish, and shrimps have been the main competitive export products of Vietnam to its main markets including US, EU and Japan. Overall, in the past few years to now, agriculture growth has maintained the rate about 4.1% annually. This growth rate must be accredited not only to the efforts of farmers but also to the works of agricultural engineers, who have provided farmers with new high yielding varieties of rice and other agricultural products. However, with the strategic plan for industrialization, the expanding of industrial zones and new cities has narrowed down the land reserves for agriculture business. In turn, this affects lives of farmers deeply and causes many problems to society, the farmers have no choice, but have to adapt with the new way of living without a proper preparation for the changes.

1.2.1.2 Industry

Prior to the "Doi Moi", under the central planned economy, the industry of Vietnam was divided into two models. The first one is the industrial firm, which was established and totally controlled and managed by the State. The second one is handicraft cooperative, which was formed base on traditional handicraft villages with the control and management by the State. Most of the output of industrial firms and handicraft cooperative were collected and distributed solely by the State. Only a very small amount of handicraft cooperative's products were allowed to sell to traditional open markets in the countryside. Under this economic regime, both industrial sectors and handicraft cooperatives were not growth. During this period, the living of people was quite difficult. This problem even become more serious when supports from the former Soviet Union and Eastern Europe countries were lessen and lessen due to their own economic problems. Under heavy pressures, the government has to change its economic system to the open market economy. This reformation allows foreign investors and private investors to create their own businesses. Since the end of 1980s, the economy has experienced the establishment of different forms of economic entities.

The end of 1980s and the early 1990s, the economy of Vietnam experienced the breaking of almost all handicraft cooperatives and signals for privatization of many SOEs. Members of the dissolved handicraft cooperative were transformed into small family businesses. The transformation is like a big rain drop down to the dry land. After a long time, people have choices and firms have to find ways to satisfy their customers' needs. The living has been much better. However, soon firms started finding out that lack of technology and short of skilled human capital significantly hinder the development and growth of their businesses.

Since the late 1990s, when the privatization law has been enacted and corporate law has been launched since the year 2000, industrial sector has been growing fast. Not only, these laws have privatized many SOEs, they also stimulated the growth of private business sector, and attracted more foreign investments. New business market and competitive labor cost attracted giant firms, such as Toyota, Honda, Canon, Intel and others to establish their own manufacturing in Vietnam. Despite fast growth, most of the industrial businesses have invested in low and medium technology. Partial reason comes from lack of skilled human capital and inadequate level of technology. Even though, majority of industrial firms have been focused on low and medium technology, they are still very important for the economic growth, as table 1.1 provides that industrial businesses contributed about 58% of the total economic output for the whole country in 2009. Among the industrial businesses, manufacturing businesses annually generated a total value in between 82% and 85% of the total industrial outputs in the period of 2006 to 2010 (GSO, 2011). In the same period, while the distribution of shares in industrial outputs of foreign firms[3] had been quite stable around 44%, SOE[4] and non SOE firms had experienced a drop in their shares from 25% to 18.5% for SOE firms and an increase from 31.1% to 38.4% for none SOE firms. These figures correctly reflect the increase in the FDI in the period of 1991 to 2009 (*see figure 1.1*) and the strategic implementation of the privatization plan.

Figure 1.1 FDI inflow in the period of 1991-2009

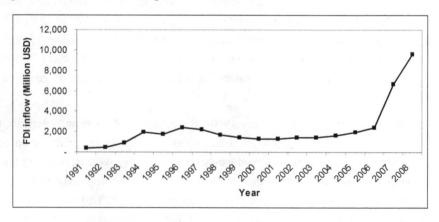

Source: UNCTAD(2009)

---

[3] GSO (2011) defined foreign business as firms that are wholly or partly owned by foreign investors.
[4] GSO (2011) defined non state business as firms that are not 100% SOE or having foreign share.

Although, there had been an increasing amount of FDI over the period, most of foreign firms had invested in low and medium low technology industry, such as garment and textile industry. As the consequence, the generated economic values from these low and medium low technology products could not make the economy booming.

Another attempt of the government, which has been implemented over the last decade, needs to be mentioned here. That is the outbreak of industrial zones, which had been observed in period of the late 1990s to 2008. The term "industrial zone" is quite different with "industrial district", which was suggested by Belussi (1999)[5] in term of divergence of business sectors. In some location, authorities have tried to encourage family businesses in handicraft villages move into industrial zones. However, most of these attempts were unsuccessfully. Causes of these failures come from both authorities and individual businesses. As the authorities in some locations do not understand the important reason of putting firms in the same sector or supporting sector close to each other, this not only helps firms to expand the distribution network, resource allocation, but also wastage management. In some other locations, authorities understand these problems, but there are not enough firms in the same sector, which would like to rent the lots. So in exchange for the principles of the industrial zone, the authorities allow different firms in different sectors to locate in the zone for the rents. Consequently, most of the industrial zones have problems with wastage management, distribution network and resource allocation. Even worst, few of them have been abandoned for years without any operation. As family businesses in Vietnam are often small size firms, which generate not much income, so they need to be cost effective to compete with a divergence of similar products in the market. Hence, moving their businesses to industrial zone is not a good option for them.

Another important economic entity in Vietnam is the handicraft village. Statistical data shows that by 2009 there have been about 2900 handicraft villages, which employed about 14 million workers (Vu, Le and Nguyen, 2010). Most of their products mainly serve domestic market. Some products have also been able to export internationally. Export value of the year 2009 reached 1 billion dollars. That is the positive sight of this economic entity. However, the negative effect has also been a

---

[5] Industrial sector was defined as "an isolated aggregation of small firms belonging to a specific sector".

headache problem for the authorities and local people living there. In a survey of 52 handicraft villages in 2011, their nature environments were evaluated as high degradation. Employees often work in harsh environment, such as 95% of them working in the dusty environment, 85.9% working in high temperature environment and 59.6% of them working in the hazardous environment.

The overall picture of the industrial sectors and handicraft is not quite positive, even though they have contributed a major portion of the national economic value and created jobs for society. The above facts imply that authorities should find ways to create a better business environment and develop pools of high quality human resources for the firms.

1.2.1.3 Trade and service

In the early years of the economic reform, Vietnam has strengthened and enhanced its relationships with many countries in the World, including US. Since then Vietnam has become member of ASEAN, APEC and most notably it has officially become a member of the WTO in the early 2007. Joining those organizations makes Vietnam become a hub in a giant global network, where businesses flow and knowledge spills over. As the result, the value of trade and service generated in 2009 increases almost two and half time of the amount contributed in 2005. Although, having impressive growth rate, trade and service businesses in Vietnam are still considered at a premature state.

According to GSO(2011), in 2009, about 84.2% of the economic value, which was generated by trading and service business, was contributed by non state business sectors, whereas foreign business generated only 2.7%. Although, economic contribution by house hold business has been slightly decreased, it still plays a very important role in the economy, as in the year 2009 they contributed nearly 50% of the total economic value, which was generated by trading and service business sector. Notably, private business sector has steadily raised its contribution over the years. The contributed amount, which was accounted for only 22.5% in 2005, reached to about 34.8% of the total economic value in 2009.

As the above paragraph mentioned that about 50% of the economic value in trade and service had been generated by house hold business, it explains why cash transaction is still very common method in Vietnam. Moreover, in contribution to the above explanation, lack of integration within the banking system and between banking systems and other services has created weaknesses and business disadvantages in financial system. Consequently, this system has been incapable of providing sophisticated services to its customers leading to entry barriers for many businesses, including ecommerce. Furthermore, traditional trading method is still applied for most of the trading partners. Face to face meetings is more favorable in comparison to other types of communication between partners. Lack of information services, leading to problems in identifying credited trading partners, hence personal network has become the most important factor in selecting trading partners in Vietnam (Steer and Sen, 2010).

1.2.2 Institutions

1.2.2.1 Institutional reform and its impacts

As mentioned above, this period marked with important changes at the top administrative levels and the issuances of new laws, which are initially served as the driving force for the development and growth of Vietnam economy. Steer and Sen (2010) provided that introduction of Corporation law in the year 2000 and the development of legislation on non-discriminatory regime on public and private firms had a increased number the Non-SOE firms in Vietnam almost 50 times in comparison to the year 1992. Figure 1.2 provides that total number of firms in Vietnam in 2009 was about 248,847 firms, which are about 5 folds of total number of firms in the year 2000.

Figure 1.2 Registered firms in Vietnam in the period of 2000-2009

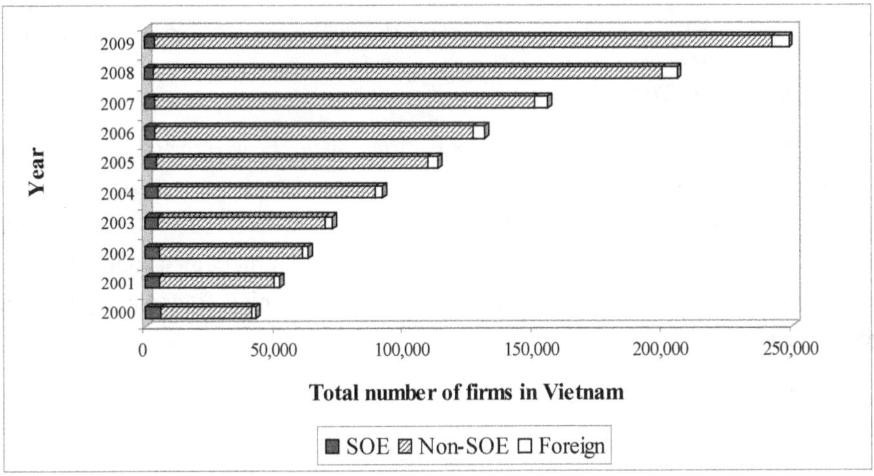

Source: GSO(2011)

With the introduction of privatization law by the National Assembly, many SOEs have been forced to privatize to create fairer competitions and reduce centralized management from the State. Moreover, SOEs, which have been generating losses for long period of times and having inefficient operations, were forced either to dissolve or merge. As the consequence, numbers of SOEs have been decreased dramatically. Statistical data shows that in 2009, total SOEs were about 3,369 firms, which are accounted for only about 40% of total SOEs in the year 2000 and there would be more SOEs to be privatized or dissolved (see table 1.2). At the same time, different incentive policies, such as tax reduction, privilege in land usage, and competitive labor costs have attracted foreign investors. In comparison to the year 2000, total recorded foreign firms in the year 2009 was about 5,625 firms, which increased about 5.3 times.

Table 1.2 Registered firms and their distributions

Year	2006		2007		2008		2009	
Unit	No.	%	No.	%	No.	%	No.	%
No. SOE	3,706	3	3,494	2.2	3,286	1.6	3,369	1.4
No. Non-state enterprise	123,392	94	147,316	94.6	196,776	95.7	238,932	96.0
No. Foreign investment enterprise	4,220	3	4,961	3.2	5,626	2.7	6,546	2.6
Total	**131,318**	100	**155,771**	100	**205,688**	100	**248,847**	100

Source: GSO(2011)

Under intense competitions, many firms have been created but a huge percentage of firms also have been closing down due to losses or inefficient operations. Steer and Sen (2010) provided that there were about 100,000 firms, which had been created in the period of 2000 to 2010, but half of them died soon after their establishments. Undeniable facts indicate that those remaining firms have generated good revenues (see figure 1.3).

Figure 1.3 Revenue earned by types of firms in period of 2000 to 2009

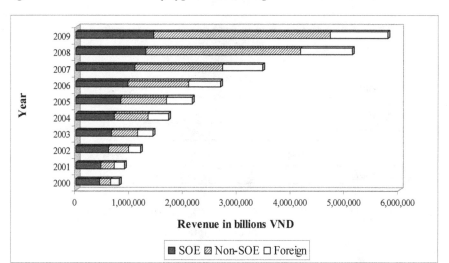

Source: Statistic Year Book (2011)

Figure 1.4 provides that SOEs still play very important role in the economy, as their economic contribution has been accounted for about 35% of the total GDP. However, the privatization strand has made the contribution of SOEs to the GDP gradually declining. Having the highest share in the contribution to GDP, Non-SOEs have reconfirmed their crucial roles in generating economic values. However, these contributions have still been marginal in comparison to their capacities. Foreign firms have contributed only about 19% of the GDP, but they have been operating more effectively.

The above figures suggest that business condition in Vietnam has been impressively improved. However, the institutional development seemly can not keep up with the development and growth of the businesses. As the consequence, businesses have been grown heterogeneously that lead to such a short lives of many businesses. Not only does this development and growth affect investors' financial capacity, but it also reduces the credit of people on the government. These weaknesses need to be identified and systematically corrected. So, further reform is essential to create a better business environment and fairer competitions.

Figure 1.4 Firms' economic contribution to GDP

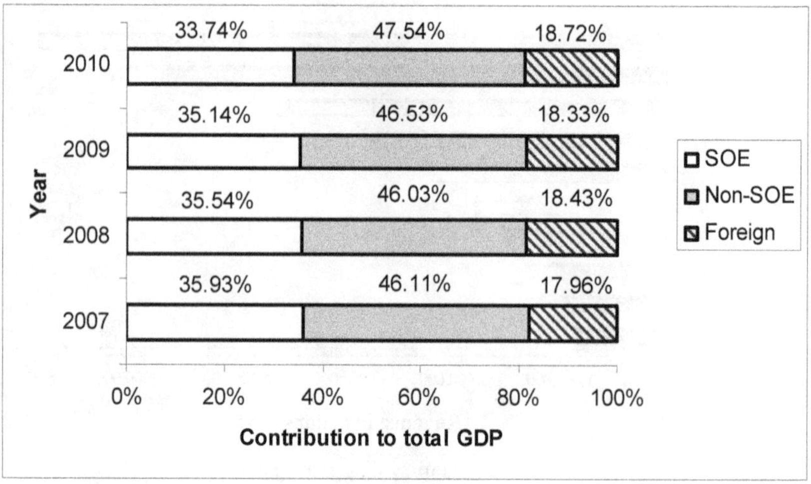

Source: Statistic Year Book (2011)

1.2.2.2 Weakness of Vietnam's institution

The institutional system of Vietnam has been viewed as a very complicated system in the sense of overlapping and contradicting of laws and regulations at different levels (Steer and Sen, 2010). Inconsistence and high rate of unfair judgment, which lead to low confidence in court system, have been observed. As McMillan and Woodruff (1999) mentioned that only 10% of managers of firms in Vietnam believed in the judgment of court. In the 2004 survey of Steer and Sen (2010), 40% of respondents said that they would not think legal contracts could be enforced in court.

Moreover, complication in procedure to file a law suit has lead to high rate of firms and individuals to look for alternative ways to settle conflicted issues. As the consequence, these firms and individuals have to rely on their own business networks, including politicians, business associations, and even criminal gangs. There is no statistical data recorded for business settlement through those conventional activities, but there has been a growing trend in using criminal gangs to settle business disputes.

Additionally, weakness of the institution is also reflected through the enforcement system, which is believed inefficient and ineffective. The rate of recidivism is very high. There have been several explanations for this phenomenon. First of all, it is about the law itself. There exist some conflicting and contradicting rules and regulations that make authorities could not handle the problem effectively. Furthermore, administrative fines, which have been introduced, may create unfair judgments and possible for corruption. Moreover, the amount of fines is often small, if the case is not prosecuted. So to many people, administrative fine is just simply an extra expense for the business.

1.2.3 Higher Education and Science and Technology

1.2.3.1 Higher education system and market

Prior to the reformation, education system in Vietnam was functionally divided. Roles of university and institution had been clearly defined (Tran and Nguyen, 2011). The university was responsible for training and the institution was responsible for doing research. There were only 9 universities through out the country, and each of those universities was designed to serve only one big dimension of the public activities. Hence, the university could have only admitted a limited number of students. Consequently, the gross enrollment had been less than 2%, leading to intense competition to get in the universities. Even 5 years after the reformation, in the academic year 1992-1993 gross enrollment could barely reach 2% (World Bank, 2008).

Market economy has opened opportunities for businesses, but also enlarged education market. Universities and research institutions have expanded their functionalities to all areas: training; researching; consulting. More and more students could enroll into universities, and institutions through many forms of training activities. According to the World Bank (2008), in the academic year 2006-2007 the gross enrollment reached 13%. As demands for education have been increased, many universities and colleges have been established in the period of 2004 to 2008.

Figure 1.5 Number of universities and colleges in the period of 2000-2010

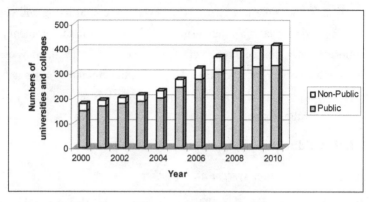

Source: GSO(2011)

Figure 1.5 indicates that there is a growing trend in both public and non public universities and colleges in the period of 2005 to 2007, and at peak, the growth rate of total number of universities and colleges reached 20% (GSO, 2011). However, there have been increasingly complaints from business sectors on the quality of education and training. The education and training have been apart from reality. Recently, the government has established a new model "university in industry" or "university in corporation". There are a number of universities including the Vietnam Petroleum University, which have been established under this model. This means that there will be more universities and colleges in the near future. This fast growth rate has created suspicions about the quality of education, especially when the existing universities and colleges have been facing with poor infrastructures and high rate of student lecturer ratio.

Despite fast growing trend in both number of public and private universities and colleges, an increasing in amount of joint operating programs between universities and colleges in Vietnam with foreign education partners have been launched. By 2010, there have been more than 115 joint collaboration programs have been legally launched in Vietnam. Even though, the tuition fee to participate in those programs can be ranged from 5 to 20 times higher than the domestic programs, the demand has been still very high.

1.2.3.2 Quality of education

In recently years, in many academic conferences, Vietnamese scholars have described lecturers as "teaching machines" or "teaching workers". This means that many of them do not have opportunities to do research or consultation while teaching. On average, the student lecturer ratio in the period of 2000 to 2008 was about 28.2 to 1, which is quite high in comparison to many countries in the world. This ratio can be much higher in the leading universities of Vietnam; for example the ratio at National Economics University is about 70 to 1. Additionally, poor infrastructures and shortage of teaching materials have been big barriers in improving the quality of education. Tran (2006) mentioned that many universities still use equipments and teaching materials dated back from the 1960s and 1970s. Most of the universities do not have an online library, and very few of them have been able to provide students to access to international journal databases. Apparently, this not only limits their research skills, but also create wider gap to the world knowledge.

Furthermore, quality of education is also reflected through the linkage between universities and industries. These linkages can be understood in two ways: providing human resources; providing research work. Looking back to the time prior to the economic reform, the linkages between universities, colleges with industries had been very clear, because the universities had been created with purpose to provide these industries both human capital and research activities. All of these transactions had been scheduled by the government. However, the establishment of open market system has somehow faded these linkages. This happened due to a number of possible reasons, including the following:

- Both academic institutions and SOE firms have to adjust themselves to the market economy. In which, the government has cut off partially or fully subsidies.

- Universities concentrated too much on theoretical researches, but less on applied researches.

- Universities have been working hard on modifying and building up theirs teaching curriculums to match with regional and international knowledge levels.

1.2.3.3 Science and Technology

In Vietnam, three organizations, which have been well known for their strategic operations and also their sizes and their national influences on science, technology and research, are Ministry of Science and Technology (MOST), Vietnam Academy of Science and Technology (VAST), and Vietnam Academy of

Social Science (VASS). MOST is a state management body, where they issue policies, rules and regulations relating to science and technology. Whereas, VAST and VASS are the two largest national research institutions of Vietnam. VAST is responsible for natural science and technology researches and VASS is responsible for social science researches. There are also many research and development organizations under line of different ministries, provinces, and cities through out Vietnam (see figure 1.6 for details).

The budget, which has been reserved for R&D, is still very small and segmented. Statistical data shows that the R&D budget had been accounted for about 0.5% to 0.6% of GDP, which were about 5 to 7 times less than the neighboring countries (Malaysia, Singapore...etc.). However, even with such small amount of budget, this source of fund has not been utilized appropriately. Nguyen (2011) mentioned that partial budget was spent irrelevantly to other fields of science and technology. Moreover, a large percentage of the budget could not be used due to irrelevant activities. Fact data shows that in 2009, Hanoi and Ho Chi Minh city received a budget of 200 billions dong and 300 billions dong respectively for science and technology researches. However, they spent just only a little more than 10% of the budget. This could mean that science and technology research has not been actively performed in these two largest cities of Vietnam. Shortage and aging science and technology researchers (Bezanson, Oldham and Tran, 2000) have been a major problem for science research in Vietnam.

Figure 1.6 Vietnam's government R&D system in 2000s.

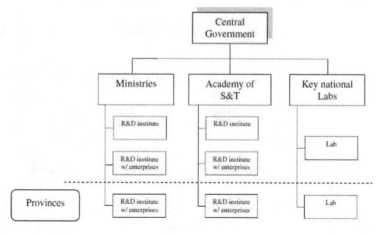

Source: (Tran T., Daim T., Kocaoglu D., 2011)

1.3 Research objectives limitation and structure of dissertation

Since the reformation of the economy, Vietnam has consensually pursued its industrialization plan. Innovation is a critical success factor for the process of industrialization, which enable economics growth. Up to now, there has not been any research studying about firms' innovation in Vietnam. To fulfill the purpose of this dissertation, this research focuses on three major areas: innovation competencies; patenting cost; IPR protection, which have been empirically and scientifically discussed in various researches by economists around the world. Therefore, the objectives of this research are to identify: the manufacturing firms' characteristics and factors that support innovation; the effects of patenting cost on patenting behaviors; the effects of IPR enforcement. Figure 1.7 introduces the flow and major research goals in each of the above specified objectives.

Apparently, figure 1.7 depicts that this dissertation contains five chapters. The first chapter provides general information on: key economics indicators, institutional framework, education and science & technology, which explain the development state of Vietnam. As most of the countries in the world, economic contributions are stemmed from agriculture, industry and trading and services. In Vietnam, large amounts of economic values have been notably contributed by manufacturing firms of industry sector. Therefore, through out this dissertation, this research mainly focuses on manufacturing firms' innovation. Furthermore, institutional system plays an important role in shaping behaviors of a society, including its economic entities, and it is also either motivating or discouraging innovation. So it is important to realize the strengths and the weaknesses of the institutional system. Additionally, education and science & technology are both knowledge and human capital generators. This means that the ability to innovate is also heavily depended on the advancement of education and science & technology. In short, this chapter provides a general picture of the economic, institutional and educational environment in Vietnam that helps judging process in the following chapters.

Identifying firms' characteristics, that support innovation, is important for authorities. Especially, in transitional phases, Vietnam has a diversity of business entities, including the three types: State Owned Enterprise (SOE); None SOE; Foreign investment firms. The contributions of these types of economic entities are very important for the growth of economy. Therefore, in chapter 2, it is vital to identify innovative manufacturing firms and their characteristics to provide suitable policies to enhance and leverage innovations in these firms. A vast amount of literatures have measured firms' innovation through patent counts, which have been widely accepted by many researchers through out decades. Probit econometric function is utilized to analyze two sources of data (World Bank data and our own survey data). The outcomes of this analysis indicate firms' characteristics and firms' competencies that stimulate firms' innovation. As the result, authorities can rely on these firms' characteristics and firms' innovation competencies to tailor their policies to support firms in achieving further optimum outcomes.

As this research mentioned above, patent has been widely used by researchers in measuring innovation. So, chapter 3 examines carefully the patenting scheme of the developing ASEAN countries with a focus on patenting cost and patent quality. Evidences have found that cheaper of patenting cost would increase the demand for patent (de Rassenfosse and van Pottelsberghe, 2010). If this is also true for these ASEAN countries, then patenting cost can be a tool for authorities to consider in making policies to encourage firms to patent more. However, the cost for patenting must be balancing with the patent quality, since there is a suspicion on the adverse relationship between the two.

Furthermore, firms' innovation is also effected by IPR enforcement in different aspects and at different magnitudes. Since the principle of IPR enforcement is to protect intellectual assets from infringements. IPR enforcement is eventually enhancing innovation. So in chapter 4, it is worth to examine the IPR enforcement system in Vietnam and compare it to the IPR enforcement of France and US. Such comparison would signal strengths and weaknesses of Vietnamese IPR enforcement system, which can be vital for authorities. Further analysis, which uses a collection of 40 summarized infringement cases and one comprehensive case, is needed to support arguments on the strengths and weaknesses of the IPR enforcement system.

Finally, chapter 5 provides a summary of key findings of the previous chapters. Suggestions are provided as recommendations to authorities for considerations. These include suggestions for short term and long term development. In short term, a quick fix in administrative measure is essential. However, in a longer term, a strategic actions and commitment of authorities are critical to: improving education and training system; providing a mechanism to allow firms to collaborate with research institutions in developing new products or new services; providing a systematic training to administrative staff and judges, whose jobs involve with the knowledge of IP; reengineering the enforcement processes to make judicial procedures become more familiar to people and gradually it should become the central resolution for all disputes, including infringements.

This research takes the opportunity to explore only the biggest economic contributor (industry) among the three (agriculture; industry; trade and service). Moreover, patent is not a perfect indicator for firms' innovation. There are many innovative products and innovative processes are not patented for many reasons. So, wider and deeper research can also be performed.

Figure 1.7 Flow and structure of dissertation

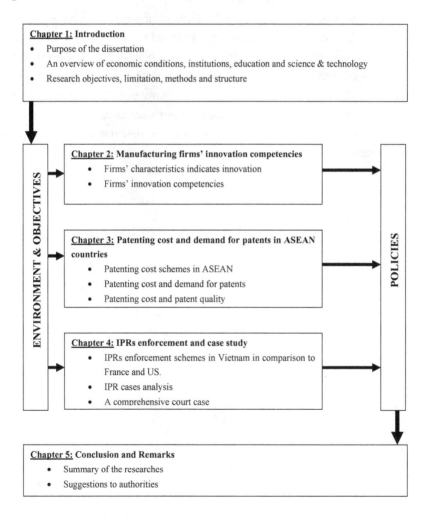

CHAPTER 2. MANUFACTURING FIRMS' INNOVATION COMPETENCIES

Objectives:

The "Doi Moi" has changed the business environment in Vietnam for almost two decades. The spill over of technology, knowledge, business law and regulation has pushed the economy to a higher stage. In order to make the economy growth in a sustainable way, firms in Vietnam need to be innovative. Although, using patent to represent firms' innovation output has been controversially argued, it is widely accepted amongst researchers. This research uses patent as the measurement tool to assess the innovation characteristics and identify the determinants that significantly influence manufacturing firms' innovation.

2.1 Introduction

Since the "Doi Moi" in 1986, the government has urged firms and organizations to change to adapt with the new open market economy. Although the government has managed to make the economy growth, the economic condition is still not very positive. In general the national export value is still much less than the national import value. Most of the export products are relating to natural resources, low tech or handicraft products. Furthermore, the country has also been facing problems with inflation, which is often higher than the growth rate. As mentioned in the first chapter, a major portion of the economic value has been generated by industrial sector. That explains why the development and growth of industrial sector has been placed in the top list of the government's action plan. The government has urged firms to be innovative to compete in domestic and foreign markets.

As innovation is the driver for business development and growth, its concepts, models have been increasingly researched since the last two decades. However, the concept of innovation is still very new in Vietnam and it has increasingly become a hot topic in both science and social research conferences, especially when Vietnam has officially become a member of the WTO in the beginning of 2007. Through these researches and conferences, Ministry of Science and Technology (MOST) and Vietnam Chamber of Commerce and Industry (VCCI) have increasingly urged firms to be innovative. Supporting to these activities, authorities have created different programs, projects to leverage the knowledge and understanding of firms on innovation, intellectual property (IP) and intellectual property rights (IPRs). In this direction, this research looks for indicators which can be utilized to distinguish innovative firms from the industry. Furthermore, it also determines factors, which influence firm innovation.

With these objectives, this analysis is organized into four parts. The first part of this research presents different concepts of innovation and different acceptable ways of measuring it. The second part makes use of the mapping innovation process of Peeters and van Pottelsberghe (2003) to design and measure firm innovation characteristics and competencies. Following that, the third part not only provides basic descriptive statistics about the sample, but they also provide empirical findings about the characteristics of innovative firms and the factors which influence firms' innovative capacity. Finally, the conclusion wraps up the findings and provides suggestions to authorities for considerations in making such policies to match with the firms' needs.

2.2 Innovation, innovation models and how innovation was measured

2.2.1 Definitions and categorization of innovation

The human civilization links to innovative activities, which have been reflected in all aspects of culture, society and science. However, the concept of innovation has just been studied systematically and scientifically since the early decades of the 20th century. The economist, Schumpeter is probably the pioneer, who firstly built the ground for discussion and theories on innovation. In his first theory that has been well known as "Schumpeter Mark I", Schumpeter (1934) provided that innovation is a combination of new or existing knowledge, resources, equipments, processes or market. Most often, the combination has been initiated by entrepreneurs. Therefore, in this theory the role of entrepreneur is very important for the development of innovation. This theory has attracted scholars in different fields, as the result, thousands of researches on innovation have been published in different journals. Amongst them, Damanpour and Evan (1984) thought that an innovation is reactions of firms to changes in the business environment. Whilst, Dosi (1988) expressed that innovation is a process of exploring and learning new product, process and organization. Although, there have been different definitions and thoughts about innovation, the principle can be understood as: "Innovation is creating something new and implementing it successfully at a market." (Brown and Ulijn, 2004). In brief, most of scholars have consented in their researches that new product or process has been stemmed from the process of transforming new ideas to new products to be commercializing or new processes to be implementing vastly in markets.

Sometimes, the definition of innovation and invention can be confused. However, Fagerberg (2007) has distinguished the two definitions separately and an invention is understood simply as a new idea for a new product or process, where as innovation is the occurrence of a new product or process in the market. More specifically, Dunphy et al. (1996) expressed that invention could be stemmed from new ideas rising from existing or new technologies. The process to turn an invention into innovation needs knowledge, capacity, skills, infrastructure, market, distribution system and financial capacity. Looking at different view, product innovation or process innovation is the added value of invention (Dunphy, 1996).

The increasing amount of scientific papers on innovation crossing different fields indicates the interest of scholars over the world on innovation, so categorization of innovation will help to better understand the nature of innovation and factors that influence new products or processes. The gained knowledge will help to ensure the success of the new product or process on the market. In accordance to the Schumpeter I and Schumpeter II, innovation is categorized into radical innovation and incremental innovation. Radical innovation is understood as basic change and not relying on any existing technology, while incremental innovation is relied on an existing technology with an aim to improve the efficiency or functionality of the product or process. Looking at the aspect of continuity and inheritance, radical innovation does not have these characteristic, while these two attributes are important for incremental innovation.

In the view of an entrepreneur, Schumpeter (1934) clarified these types of innovation into five sub-types of innovation, as the bellow:

1. introduction of a new product or a qualitative change in an existing product;

2. process innovation new to an industry;

3. the opening of a new market;

4. development of new sources of supply for raw materials or other inputs;

5. changes in industrial organization

After the attempt of Schumpeter, many scholars have tried to redefine and classify innovation in different ways. Amongst them, Kline and Rosenberg (1986), Trott (1988) and Bell and Pavitt (1993) mentioned that innovation was the general term for any of product innovation, process innovation, organizational innovation, production innovation, commercial/marketing innovation, service innovation or all of them. Furthermore, Damanpour (1991) classified innovation into two major classes: technical innovation and administrative innovation. Technical innovation was then defined as a type of innovation, which is the super set of product innovation, process innovation and service innovation, whereas administrative innovation comprises any of a new procedure, a new policy, and a new organizational form. Trott (1998) categorized innovation even further, so innovation can be any type of product innovation, process innovation, organizational innovation, production innovation, commercial/marketing innovation or service innovation. In a more open thought, (Fagerberg et al., 2004).suggested that innovation does not need to be new globally, it can be new locally as long as it is fitted to the local context.

In different approach, not only do Henderson and Clark (1990) look at the ways how components of a product or a process are built, but also how they are integrated. According to the author, if innovation is only classified into the radical innovation and incremental innovation that will be hard to explain some unsuccessful innovations, even though they are considered obvious. Xerox can be an example that illustrates the above argument, as Xerox can be proud of the technical leadership in producing Photocopy machines. However, it was not successful in developing mini photocopy machines. So, the author has classified innovation into four types (see figure 2.1): radical innovation; incremental innovation; modular innovation; architecture innovation. Amongst them, radical innovation is understood as a kind of innovation, not only does that influence very much on the knowledge of building components of a new product or a new process, but it also provides a new way of linking modules together. In another extreme, the incremental innovation does not require much change in the knowledge of creating and linking the modules. On the other hand, the modular innovation does not ask for much change in the knowledge of linking modules, but it requires much change in the knowledge of creating the module. In opposite, the architecture innovation focus more on the link between modules, but it relaxes on the knowledge of creating the module.

Figure 2.1: Henderson and Clark innovation model

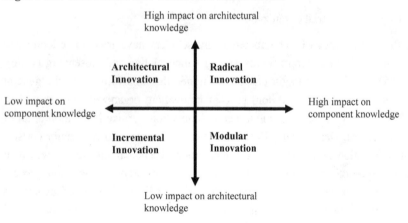

Source: Henderson and Clark (1990)

Technology innovation plays an important role in leverage the productivity, alleviation the hazard, improvement of work safety, environmental protection and raising the quality of life. A recent research of Lee (2010) emphasized that technical innovation brings economic benefits more than any other investment that pours into the company's operation. Furthermore, technology innovation often comes with patents, which can be used to indirectly measure the innovativeness of firms. Therefore, in this research context, we concentrate on innovation process to identify the factors that influence firms' innovation.

2.2.2 Innovation models

2.2.2.1 Abernathy and Utterback Innovation Model

Abernathy and Utterback (1978) have built a model of innovation, which integrates both product innovation and process innovation in a competitive environment. This broad picture shows how product and process innovation are initiated and developed. Figure 2.2 clearly shows that the model comprises of three phases: fluid phase; transitional phase; specific phase. In the fluid phase, innovative activities can be exciting with many new ideas. However, the concept of the product is not clear, so as the customers' needs. So, new product is often produced by high skilled employees with general purpose machines through different processes. These pilot products are launched out to the market with a mission to validate the market's needs. Often, at this stage, the market for these products is also uncertain. When a new product seemingly responses to the market needs, many other producers can imitate the idea and invent different processes to reproduce the product. In such circumstance, the product enters the transitional phase. As the new technology becomes more mature and the needs of the market are getting clearer, more fierce competitions will be expected. The outcome of these competitions is a dominant design, which shapes the future development of the product. Furthermore, when the dominant design is defined, firms often try to follow the design to stay connect in the network. The phase wraps up with new processes and specialized machines that enable mass production. After the appearance of the dominant design, firms enter into specific phase, where producers mainly focus on improving product performance and lowering the cost for producing products.

The model of Abernathy and Utterback provides development strands of product innovation and process innovation through phases. Understanding each phase clearly would help firms take appropriate actions to make product or process innovation stay competitive. However, Abernathy and Utterback model does not completely show external factors, which are critically influencing each phase of product or process innovation.

Figure 2. 2: Abernathy and Utterback innovation model

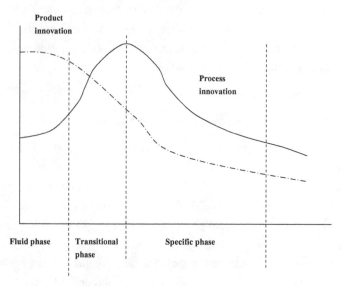

Source: Abernathy and Utterback (1978)

2.2.2.2 The mapping process of innovation

As the model of Abernathy and Utterback only provide an overall picture of innovation development, some other scholars have also been attempting to define the innovation process. Amongst the scholars, Pavitt (2004) have suggested that innovation process comprised of three overlapping sub-processes: the production of knowledge; the transformation of knowledge into products, systems, processes and services; and the continuous matching to the future market demands. Inheriting other scholars' works, Peeters and Van Pottelsberghe have produced a mapping for innovation process that describes in details the steps in developing an innovative product. Furthermore, factors that influence the innovation development are also indicated clearly. As illustrating in the figure 2.3, the innovative product of a firm started with ideas generation, then ideas implementation and the dissemination of new products or process to market. Not only are these processes bounded by firm innovative culture, but they are also very much influenced by external source of information and the barriers to innovation. This mapping provides a clear picture of product innovation and their related processes that would help managers and scholars in evaluating the innovative capacity of firms.

Figure 2.3: Mapping the innovation process

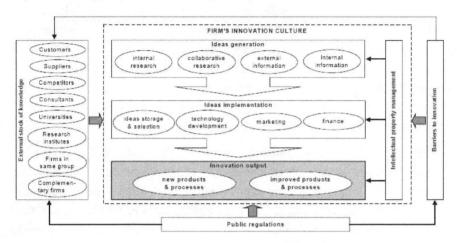

Source: Peeters and Van Pottelsberghe (2003)

2.2.3 Measuring innovation

In the previous discussion, this dissertation has emphasized on the important role of innovation to the development and growth of economy. That also explain why, measuring innovation have attracted attention of many researchers around the globe. The measurement of innovation might have been started since the early 20th century, when economic historians and sociologists recognized the advantages of presenting innovative phenomenon in case studies and monograph. However the limitation of case studies remains in the question of representativeness with confidence. Casper (2005) mentioned that quantitative surveys can be designed to be representative. As in the early 1990s, French and Italians have done extensive surveys on innovation. The French survey of innovation in 1991 has still been considered as the most extensive and the most representative, as it covered 30,000 enterprises of all business sectors (Debresson, 1996).

Another measuring approach, which has been implemented, is to utilize journals and field experts and then launch an industrial survey. Freeman and Townsend are the pioneers in this field. To carry out this kind of survey, different sources of related journals and questions are carefully designed for different sectors and then sent to different experts in their matching sectors to identify significant innovation. Then the information is validated with the relevant firms and graded by experts (Debresson, 1996).

A standardized way of presenting questions to different industries and business sector were first discussed and published in the Oslo manual of OECD in 1992. Then in 1993 EUROSTAT and OECD together launched standardized questionnaires to most EU countries through the Community Innovation Survey (CIS). This kind of survey is very interesting in the way, it allows international and inter industry comparisons. In the late 1990s and beginning of 2000s, the raising questions on the identification and measurement of competencies that are the driving forces of firms' innovation process were challenged many researchers.

In the past decade, many researchers have used the standardized questionnaires or adopted versions to study about innovation in firms around the world. However, there have been controversies on standardization of dependent and independent variables in the measurement. As de Rassenfosse and van Pottelsberghe (2009) provided that there had not widely known accepted direct method to measure innovation performance. Some of the measurement relied on either earnings or total factor productivity growth. Several other authors have used sales of new products or improved products as a criterion to measure innovation (Brouwer and Kleinknecht, 1999). Although, most often Sale may represent well the innovative capacity of firms, there are cases, where sale is well influenced by the economics system, the sophistication of the market system, and the coverage of network of distribution system...etc.

Another strand in measuring innovative capacity of firms has been acknowledged and there have been an increasing number of researchers use patent count as a way to measure technological innovation. This method has been widely accepted amongst researchers. However, Lanjouw and Schankerman (2004) suggested that patent count and patent quality are in inverse relationship. There have been suspicions on quality of patents in countries, where patent inflation is observed. Moreover, in countries, where IPR system is weak, registration for patent grant is for recognition rather than protection (Lipsey and Carlaw, 1998), so patent count also does not reflect exact state of the technological innovation.

Probably the controversy on measuring innovative capacity would be never ended. It is just the matter, which method is more reliable and feasible to reflect the innovative competencies of firms. Because, there are existing many loop holes in the accounting system of Vietnam, financial figures may be not correctly reflected well firms' performance. Therefore, this dissertation uses the probability of having a patent to measure firms' innovation. Manufacturers contribute a major portion of the

GDP, hence measuring innovation of these firms will be meaningful, as the outcomes would assist policymakers in making appropriate policies that support the development and growth of the innovative firms.

2.3 Research questions and survey design

2.3.1 Research questions

As presented in the previous section, the economics of Vietnam has rapidly changed since the last couple of decades. Manufacturing firms have played an important role in leveraging the economics and contributed a large portion of the GDP. Moreover, the economy has also experienced the rising in number of patent filings, although the amount is still small. As mentioned above, patent count is reflecting the firms' innovation and it can be used to measure firms' innovativeness. It is important to identify the characteristics of innovative firms and factors that influence firms' innovation. This identification is important for policymakers in consideration for issuing such policies that stimulate firms' innovativeness. Many daunting questions have been raised in the last decade, amongst them, such question like "What kind of policies will promote innovation?" and "will university-industry linkage stimulate innovation?" These questions have been increasingly discussed in many separate conferences, which were organized by Vietnam Chamber of Commerce and Industry (VCCI), Ministry of Science and Technology (MOST) and Ministry of Education and Training (MOET). Learning from the previous studies of other scholars, one may notice that innovative firms have some unique characteristics. Moreover, certain factors can impact on the level of firms' innovativeness. In recognizing these characteristics and factors would be benefit for managers, partners, investors and policies makers. Therefore, this research attempts to answer the following two questions:

Research question 1: What are the firms' characteristics, which may indicate the innovativeness of a manufacturing firm in Vietnam?

Research question 2: What are the determinants, which may influence the manufacturing firms' innovativeness?

In similar to the first research question, many scholars' works have examined several characteristics of firms, which often include the size, the age and the type of firms...etc. In identifying factors that impact on the innovation of a firm, this research also relies on the mapping innovation process of Peeters and van

Pottelsberghe (2003). Because, not only this mapping provides clearly and orderly sub-processes of the innovation process, but it also points out potential factors that may importantly influence firms' innovation.

To answer the first question, a rich data set of over 1000 firms, which was collected by the World Bank in 2009, is used to analyze. However, this data set was not designed to fully match with the mapping innovation process of Peeters and van Pottelsberghe (2003). So, it can only be used to answer the first research question and partially the second research question. Therefore, extra surveys are needed to answer the second question of this research.

2.3.2 Research model and design

As discussed earlier, this dissertation utilizes the mapping innovation process to construct a model to measure firms' innovation competencies. Beside characteristics of firms that can be indicators for firm innovation. Other factors, including culture innovation, ability to generate new ideas, ability to implement new ideas, and barriers to innovation that match with the mapping innovation process, can be the determinants of firms' innovation. The rich data set of the World Bank (2009) cover more than 1000 firms crossing the country can be an ideal data source for analysis. However, some competencies, such as culture innovation and ability to generate new ideas are missing. Therefore, a separate survey should be launched to collect data for further analysis. The model can be presented as shown in figure 2.4.

A patent is only granted when it has the following three characteristics: novelty; inventiveness; and industrial capability. Based on these characteristics, patent can be used as a proxy to measure firm's innovative performance. This analysis uses patent as a dependent variable. The value of this variable, which is depended on the probability of a firm having a patent, takes value of 1 if a firm had at least 1 patent and 0 otherwise. Details of each of the variables for World Bank data set and for the Survey data set can be found in the Appendix 1a and Appendix 1b respectively.

The first part of the model includes firm characteristics (Age; Size; Legal business type; and Technology advancement), which use as control variables in the model. There have been arguments in different researches on the firm age and firm innovation. However, the findings have been mixture. As Hansen (1992) suggested that firm age was one of the determinant indicating firm's innovations. In different approach, Huergo and Jaumandreu (2004) provided that younger firms had higher probability of innovation, while Peeters and Van Potterlsberghe (2006) observed a U-shaped relationship between firm age and the probability of having a patent portfolio. In investigating the indication of firm age to firm innovation, firm age is calculated by the duration from year of firm established to the end of the year 2009.

Figure 2.4 Model of innovation measurement

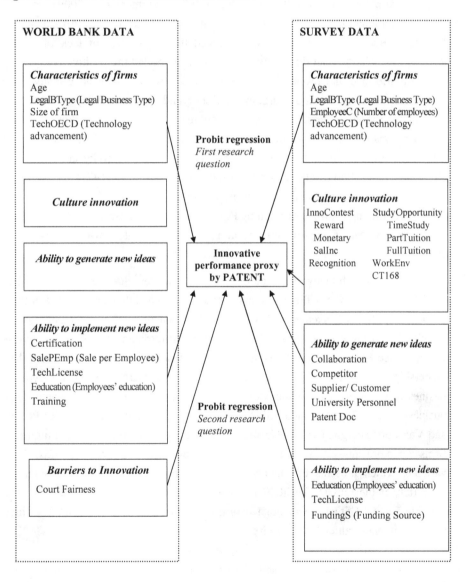

Another firm characteristic, which has been widely investigated, is the firm size[6]. With an explanation on the monopolistic power of large firm, the financial advantage and available resources, Schumpeter (1942) suggested that large firm was more innovative. This suggestion has been supported by many other researches, including Link (1981), who provided that the return on R&D is positively increased with the firm size. (Rothwell and Dodgson 1991; Rammer et al. 2009), as these authors mentioned that not only did small firms have disadvantages in financial for long term R&D, but they were also bounded to the problem of lack of human resource. Despite the fact that many authors have supported the positive relationship between firm size and propensity to innovation. However, there have many other findings opposed to the above argument. Cohen and Klepper (1996) found a little support for the above argument and these authors even pointed out that the above argument was not true for chemical sector. Even more seriously, Cohen and Klepper (1996) claimed an adverse relationship between R&D productivity and firm size. Other interesting findings have also been found by Pavitt et al. (1987), as the author claimed that large firms and small firms are more innovative than moderate size firms. This finding is also confirmed by Peeters and Van Pottelsberghe (2003). These arguments indicate that firm size is an interesting indicator, which is worth to examine.

Different with many other countries, where only few State Owned Enterprises (SOEs) are existed, the SOEs in Vietnam are still many and they are still one of three economic pillars of Vietnam. Despite the fact, businesses in Vietnam can be classified into three major types: SOEs; Foreign firms; and Non-SOEs or private firms. Since their management styles, their resource mobilization and their ownerships are different, this may be interesting to learn whether the type of businesses would indicate its innovativeness. So, a categorical variable, type of legal business (LegalBType), is included in the model. Additionally, the finding of Peeters and Van Pottelsberghe (2003) also suggested that large high tech, medium high tech firms are more innovative than small medium low tech and low tech firms. So, a variable, which presents the advancement of technology in accordance with the definition of the OECD (TechOECD) will also be included for investigation. The variable TechOECD takes value of 1 if firm is classified as high tech or medium high tech, and it takes value of 0 otherwise.

---

[6] Firm size is measured by a number of employees in the firm. It also can be classified as Small, Medium and Large.

Following the mapping innovation process of Peeters and Van Pottelsberghe (2003), this dissertation commences with the first competency, culture of innovation. Common understanding, culture is the share values, beliefs, expectation, moral, and norms in an organization, a group or society. Culture innovation may be reflected through a number of activities including the contest and their participation of firms in external activities. Moreover, incentive packages (study opportunity and reward) and the working environment play important role in motivate employees for their contributions. In the past, during the central planned economy, government and firms had organized contests for bright ideas or utility solution. This is a good way to share information and stimulate for new ideas and new or better solutions. Firms need reinforce positive contribution by rewarding employees for such innovative ideas. A small amount of money and a reward certification or an increase in the rank of salary would motivate employees to contribute more. So the variable reward and its sub-variables: monetary; increase in the rank of salary (Salinc); and recognition is integrated into the model. Each of these sub-variable would take value either Yes or No to indicate whether firm exercises the option. The variable reward is the combination of any two of the three sub-variables. The variable reward would take value of 1 if at least the two sub-variables in the three take values "Yes". Furthermore, development of human capital is always a daunting issue for innovative firm. An innovative culture would support individuals or groups of individuals to gain more knowledge and skills. Despite the fact, Johnson et al (1996) suggested that between 74% and 77% of innovative Canadian firms had provided either formal or informal training to their employees. So, literally, by providing employees with opportunities to study, firms can leverage employees' expertise leading to further innovation (Torraco and Swanson, 1995). More aggressively, not only have some firms provided study opportunities for their employees, but they also cover partially or fully tuition fees. The variable study opportunity (StudyOpp) comprises of three sub-variables: providing times for study (TimeStudy); supporting employee with tuition fees (PartTuition; FullTuition). These sub-variables take value Yes or No to present the support of firm. The variable study opportunity then takes value of 1 when any two of the sub-variables take values of "Yes" and 0 for otherwise. The affect of those activities can only be effective when it is supported by adequate infrastructure and team work environment. Therefore, a Likert scale of 1 to 5 is designed to evaluate the working environment in term of friendly. So the closer to the value of 1 is the lesser friendly of firm environment. The value of 5 means the firm environment is very friendly. To make sure that the environment is surely friendly, this analysis assigns value of 1 to the variable environment when its likert value is 4 or 5, otherwise value of the variable is set to 0. Additionally, in a different context, firms in Vietnam are not familiar with knowledge of intellectual property rights. Since 2005, the MOST has launched a national program, which has been known as program 168, to provide firms with basic knowledge on intellectual property rights. Therefore, firms, who attended the program, would be considered to have innovative culture. A variable (CT168) is designed to indicate whether firms participate in the program. So, the variable would take value of 1 when a firm has participated in the program and 0 for otherwise.

Following with the second competency, firms can generate ideas through two important sources, one is internal source and the other is external source of ideas. In this analysis the external source is focused, because of the lack of collaboration between firms and other institutions that have been acknowledged by both MOET and MOST.

As Brouwer and Kleinknecht (1996) provided that competitor, supplier and universities' personnel are significant sources of innovation. The variable collaboration, which comprises of three sub-variables competitor, supplier and universities' personnel, is designed to capture the aggressiveness of firm in collaboration for new ideas. A value of Yes is given to firm, which has initiated the relationship with any of these sources. The collaboration is then assigned a value of 1 if a firm initiated with two or more sources for new ideas, and a value of 0 for otherwise. Additionally, firm utilize the patent document should be very innovative, since patent document is a very important source for innovation. The variable (patent doc) is designed with a Likert scale of 1 to 5, where 5 means that firm very much utilizes the patent document and 1 presents for no usage of patent document. The variable takes value of 1 when it answered 4 or 5 and 0 for otherwise.

The third competency, which will be examined, is the firm ability in implementing new ideas. In a research, Cohen and Levinthal (1990) emphasized the absorptive capacity of firm on innovation. This absorptive capacity is partially reflected by the capacity of employees through their education background and the ability of firm to acquire technology licensing. Moreover, Krammer (2009) suggested that innovation requires human resource competences, which are critically depended on the level of education and training. So employee education (Eeducation) in a firm can be an important factor for measuring firm innovation. The World Bank measured the education of production employees follow a Likert scale of 1-5, where 5 mean that average employee has 13 years or more of education. So, this analysis codes employee education as 1 when firm's average employee education is 13 years and over and 0 for otherwise. For the dynamic group, the coding is based on the percentage of employees having a degree. On the other hand, technology licensing (TechLicense) get the Yes or No answer to present their ability in acquiring technology and master the technology. So if a firm gets use of a technology licensing, the variable TechLicense is set to 1 and 0 for otherwise. As always, an innovative product needs funding to turn new idea into a new product. So the ability of firm to access to different sources of fund can be very important. This analysis assigns a value of 1 to the variable funding source (fundings) when a firm answers that it can acquire funding and a value of 0 for not being able to acquire funding. Furthermore, the World Bank data includes extra two variables: certification (international certification); and formal training (training). Presumably, these variables reflect firms' ability in implementing new ideas, because their operations have been evaluated for quality assurance and their equipped knowledge and skills that have been obtained through training or knowledge spillover from foreign businesses. Firm owns an international certification gets a value of 1 for the variable certification and 0 for not having an international certification. Firm, which organizes training for its permanent and full-time employees, also gets 1 for its variable and 0 for not having training in place.

The last competency, barriers to innovation, is taken into account to assess the fairness of court system in Vietnam. As innovative products or processes should be protected against infringement, weak appropriability regime may make firms hesitate to produce new products or processes. Since the World Bank measured this variable in a Likert scale with value from 1 to 4. These values are then recoded as 1 for answers with 4 and 0 for the rests.

Since the dependent variable takes binary values (0 and 1), this analysis utilizes the probit function to identify firms characteristics which may indicate firm innovation. Furthermore, the same method is also applied to measure firm innovation through its competencies: innovative culture, ideas generation, ideas implementation, and barrier to innovation.

2.3.3 Descriptive analysis and empirical results

As described above, the analysis of firm innovation relies on the two data sources. The first data source is provided by the World Bank and the second is collected through a quick survey. World Bank data source (WBS) comes with a sample of 1,054 firms. Amongst them, about nearly 70% of firms are in manufacturing businesses. Given the scope of the analysis, which is limited to manufacturing firms, the refinement process takes out the non-manufacturing firms and missing data of the output. Finally, the WBS is left with 521 firms, which are qualified for analysis.

As described previously, the WBS does not provide data for assessing the culture of innovation, and the idea generation competencies. A quick survey was designed based on the mapping innovation process (Peeters and van Pottelsberghe, 2003) covering three major competencies: (1) Firms culture innovation; (2) External source of ideas; (3) Ability to implement ideas; (see Appendix b). Relying on this mapping, a number of related questionnaires were designed to collect the required data. Learning from past experiences, long questionnaire would decrease the response rate, so in order to increase the rate and gather reliable answers, a questionnaire was designed only in one A4 paper with less than 20 questions, which allow a respondent could answer in a short time. The questionnaires have been sent to two hundred firms, who attended the Techmart[7] 2009 exhibition in Hanoi. One hundred twenty four survey forms were returned, and only 64 forms, which are accounted for 32% of the total, could be used for analysis. Firms participate in the Techmart to introduce their new products and new technologies to potential customers. Those firms can be considered as dynamic firms. In this analysis, the WBS data can be considered as national wide data and the survey data can be assumed as data of dynamic firms.

2.3.3.1 Characteristics of firms

Following the model, the first part contains basic attributes relating to characteristics of firms, such as: age, size, legal business types and the advancement of technology (TechOECD). Table 2.1(a) provides that small size businesses dominate the WBS sample with 73.3% of firms, whereas the large and medium firms are accounted for only 10.9% and 15.7% respectively. The empirical evidences provide that the relationship between firm size and innovative output is not significant, although there are positive correlations between the two for the both data sets. Looking at the relationship between the age of firms and their innovation, as the patent is not significantly correlated with the age square, but correlated with the age at 95% significance level (see table 2.2). So the relationship follows a linear strand.

---

[7] Techmart is national wide event, where firms introduce their new products or new processes annually.

However, in the group of dynamic firms, this relationship is not significant. These outcomes are different with the U-shaped relationship, which has been found by Peeters and van Pottelsberghe (2006), or the finding of Loderer and Waelchli (2010). The differences in the finding may be explained by the change in the economic system, which has recognized private firms and foreign firms as legal economic entities and pushed the privatization processes of SOEs since the early 1990. So the firms, which have been either newly established or renewed themselves, have to adapt with the changes.

Table 2.1 Description of firms' characteristics

			SURVEY DATA							WORLD BANK DATA			
			Size							Size			
			Small	Medium	Large	Total				Small	Medium	Large	Total
Firm characteristics													
TechOECD*	LT&ML	Count	15	9	27	51	TechOECD	LT&ML	Count	345	73	51	469
		% of Total	23.4%	14.1%	42.2%	79.7%			% of Total	66.2%	14.0%	9.8%	90.0%
	HT&MH	Count	1	3	9	13		HT&MH	Count	37	9	6	52
		% of Total	1.6%	4.7%	14.1%	20.3%			% of Total	7.1%	1.7%	1.2%	10.0%
Legal Business Type**	Private	Count	11	7	14	32	Legal Business Type	Private	Count	324	54	24	402
		% of Total	17.2%	10.9%	21.9%	50.0%			% of Total	62.2%	10.4%	4.6%	77.2%
	Foreign	Count	2	1	10	13		Foreign	Count	43	17	19	79
		% of Total	3.1%	1.6%	15.6%	20.3%			% of Total	8.3%	3.3%	3.6%	15.2%
	SOE	Count	3	4	12	19		SOE	Count	15	11	14	40
		% of Total	4.7%	6.3%	18.8%	29.7%			% of Total	2.9%	2.1%	2.7%	7.7%

Source: own calculation derived from the World Bank data (2009) and own survey

* *A classification of technology advancement based on Oslo manual (OECD, 1997), technology advancement is classified into High tech (HT); Medium high tech (MH); Medium low tech (ML); and low tech (LT).*

** *Legal businesses are clarified as: Private; Foreign; State Owned Enterprise (SOE); The term Foreign includes Foreign Joint Venture, which has more than or equal to 20% of shares in a company.*

Moreover, the change has also initiated the system of intellectual property (IP) that provides firms with opportunities to file for protection of their intellectual assets. However, in this transitional period, older firms will have advantages over the younger firms in many aspects including infrastructure and networking with government agencies. Furthermore, legal business types are also found to be positive significant at 99% confident level. In such circumstance, this empirical outcome means that SOEs are considered more innovative than the other firms. However, this relationship is not confirmed for the dynamic group. As, Bhide (2000) mentioned that only 6% of new start-up firms could bring unique products to the market, while 58% of other start-up firms just brought things that already in the market. So, if it is the case for Vietnamese firms, then it would be probably very hard to tell whether the older or the younger firms are more innovative in the dynamic group. In assessing the technology advancement, low tech and medium low tech firms are accounted for the majority in both samples. Although, firms participated in the Techmart were assumed to be dynamic, nearly 80% of the firms were classified as LT&ML technology firms that is about 10% lower in comparison to the WBS. These figures reflect the fact that the percentage of firms having at least 1 patent over the last ten years is about 6.3% for country wide data and about 14.1% for dynamic firms (see table 2.1). These figures are way smaller in comparison to the firms in Belgium, as in 2003 about 64% of firms utilizes their patent portfolios for their production (Peeters and van Pottelsberghe, 2003). Empirical data provides that there is no significant confidence for the technology advancement in the World Bank data set. However, technology advancement is significant at 95% in the survey data. This implies that HT&MH tech firms are more innovative in the dynamic group.

Table 2.2 Empirical analysis for firm characteristics

WORLD BANK DATA				SURVEY DATA			
Patent	**Coef.**	**z**	**VIF**	**Patent**	**Coef.**	**z**	**VIF**
Firm characteristics							
TechOECD	-0.09056	0.29	1.01	TechOECD	1.02069	2.23**	1.07
Legal Business type	0.458653	3.54***	1.08	Legal Business type	0.10469	0.42	1.08
Size	0.043657	0.32	1.1	Size	0.28105	0.93	1.17
Age	0.01346	2.08**	1.08	Age	-0.006	0.36	1.11

Source: own calculation based on World Bank (2009) and own survey

*** Significance at 95% level of confidence*

**** Significance at 99% level of confidence*

2.3.3.2 Firm innovation culture

In assessing the innovation culture of the dynamic group, this analysis focuses on the aggressiveness of firms in acquiring new ideas, new solutions and knowledge to make firms growth. The two activities: innovation contest; and joining the program 168 were observed. Table 2.3 provides that almost half of the firms answered that they have organized the innovation contest annually, while only a little more than a third of the dynamic firms participate in the program 168. Amongst them, large LT&ML firms are quite active in these activities. However, it seems that private firms are more interesting in organizing innovation contest, while SOEs participate more on the program 168. Empirical analysis suggests that firms which actively participate in the program 168 are likely more innovative.

Table 2.3 Descriptive and empirical statistics for firms' innovation culture

SURVEY DATA			Size			
			Small	Medium	Large	Total
Culture of innovation						
Innovation contest	No	Count	7	9	15	31
		% of Total	10.9%	14.1%	23.4%	48.4%
	Yes	Count	9	3	21	33
		% of Total	14.1%	4.7%	32.8%	51.6%
Reward	No	Count	9	9	22	40
		% of Total	14.1%	14.1%	34.4%	62.5%
	Yes	Count	7	3	14	24
		% of Total	10.9%	4.7%	21.9%	37.5%
Study Opportunity	0	Count	13	10	19	42
		% of Total	20.3%	15.6%	29.7%	65.6%
	1	Count	3	2	17	22
		% of Total	4.7%	3.1%	26.6%	34.4%
Work Environment	0	Count	4	7	7	18
		% of Total	6.3%	10.9%	10.9%	28.1%
	1	Count	12	5	29	46
		% of Total	18.8%	7.8%	45.3%	71.9%
Program 168	0	Count	11	8	21	40
		% of Total	17.2%	12.5%	32.8%	62.5%
	1	Count	5	4	15	24
		% of Total	7.8%	6.3%	23.4%	37.5%

SURVEY DATA			
Patent	Coef.	z	VIF
Innovation Culture			
Innovation Contest	0.28204	0.48	1.0
Reward	1.35512	2.1**	1.0
Study Opportunity	1.79856	2.59**	1.1
Work Environment	-0.4471	-0.69	1.0
Program 168	1.27534	1.96**	1.1

Source: own survey and calculation
** Significance at 95% level of confidence
*** Significance at 99% level of confidence

Source: own survey and calculation

Innovation culture can also be seen through the way firms provide incentives for employees for their valuable contributions. Firms often provide rewards to employees to reinforce their positive contributions. Reward can be either monetary, increase in salary, certificate of recognition or any combination. Amongst them, monetary is the most common way of rewarding a firm. Commonly, firms reward their employees with a combination of those three choices, so a firm is considered as innovative when it takes a combination of choices.

Table 2.4 shows that 37.5% of the dynamic firms have rewarded their employees with two or more choices. Empirical data provides that the relationship between patent and reward is positively significance at 95%. This means that firm's reward system is important to make firm more innovative. Furthermore, firms also provide incentives to their employees with opportunities to update their knowledge and learning new things. It is very interesting to see that large LT&ML SOEs provide more study opportunities for their employees. Empirical data found that study opportunity is highly significant determinant for firm innovation.

Table 2.4 Description of firms' innovation cultures classified by technology advancement

SURVEY DATA					
			Technology Advancement		Total
			ML&LT	HT&MH	
Innovation contest	No	Count	24	7	31
		% of Total	37.5%	10.9%	48.4%
	Yes	Count	27	6	33
		% of Total	42.2%	9.4%	51.6%
Reward	No	Count	34	6	40
		% of Total	53.1%	9.4%	62.5%
	Yes	Count	17	7	24
		% of Total	26.6%	10.9%	37.5%
Study Opportunity	No	Count	37	5	42
		% of Total	57.8%	7.8%	65.6%
	Yes	Count	14	8	22
		% of Total	21.9%	12.5%	34.4%
Work Environment	No	Count	16	2	18
		% of Total	25.0%	3.1%	28.1%
	Yes	Count	35	11	46
		% of Total	54.7%	17.2%	71.9%
Program 168	No	Count	35	5	40
		% of Total	54.7%	7.8%	62.5%
	Yes	Count	16	8	24
		% of Total	25.0%	12.5%	37.5%

Source: own survey and calculation

Additionally, in this survey, about 71.9% of the firms were considered having friendly and collaborative working environment. Amongst them, large LT&ML private firms tend to have better working environment. However, empirical data suggests no significant confidence for the linkage between working environment and innovation.

2.3.3.3 Ideas generation

Innovative firms often look out for new ideas, so they aggressively seek for collaboration with competitors, suppliers and university personnel. However, in this analysis, table 2.5 provides that about 73.4% and 76.6% of firms do not collaborate with universities' personnel and competitors respectively. This indicates problems in the collaborative mechanism.

Table 2.5 Firm ability in generating new idea from external sources

			SURVEY DATA			
			Size			Total
			Small	Medium	Large	
Collaboration	No	Count	13	8	20	41
		% of Total	20.3%	12.5%	31.3%	64.1%
	Yes	Count	3	4	16	23
		% of Total	4.7%	6.3%	25.0%	35.9%
Competitor	No	Count	13	8	28	49
		% of Total	20.3%	12.5%	43.8%	76.6%
	Yes	Count	3	4	8	15
		% of Total	4.7%	6.3%	12.5%	23.4%
Supplier/ Customer	No	Count	8	6	9	23
		% of Total	12.5%	9.4%	14.1%	35.9%
	Yes	Count	8	6	27	41
		% of Total	12.5%	9.4%	42.2%	64.1%
University Personnel	No	Count	14	7	26	47
		% of Total	21.9%	10.9%	40.6%	73.4%
	Yes	Count	2	5	10	17
		% of Total	3.1%	7.8%	15.6%	26.6%

Source: own survey and calculation

As presented in the previous section, research institutions in Vietnam have been belonging to the state. Most of their research funds have been totally relied on the state's budget. In accession to this budget, research institutions have to do projects given by or proved by the state. Most of these researches have been described as unrealistic or inapplicable due to unrealistic requirements. Prior to the "Doi Moi", the linkage between research institutions and manufacturers had been enforced by the state. However, after the "Doi Moi", with the acceptance of private and foreign economic entities, the linkage between research institutions and manufacturers has been blurry. In this open market mechanism, few research institutions and individual researchers have been actively collaborating with private firms to generate new ideas for new solutions, new products or new processes.

In this analysis, firm, which has been collaborated with two or more external sources, is considered as innovative firm. Base on that table 2.6 provides that only 35.9% of firms expressed that they had collaborated two or more external sources for new ideas. Large low tech private firms likely collaborate more with external source for new ideas. Empirical data suggests that collaboration with external source of data is important to make firms innovative.

Table 2.6 Descriptive and empirical statistics for firms' collaboration with external sources of ideas.

SURVEY DATA					SURVEY DATA			
			Size					
			Small	Medium	Large	Patent	Coef.	z	VIF
Collaboration	0	Count	13	8	20	Collaboration with external sources	1.14486	2.66***	
		% of Total	20.3%	12.5%	31.3%				
	1	Count	3	4	16				
		% of Total	4.7%	6.3%	25.0%				

Source: own survey and calculation

*** Significance at 99% level of confidence

Source: own survey and calculation

Base on this, government should change the way of generating requirements and funding mechanism. The requirements should come from firms and market needs. Researchers, who have enough capacity and provide interesting ideas for these matching requirements, should be given the research fund. Since, this research fund has been initiated to solve problems for firms and market needs, therefore firms should also make contribution to this funding source. The whole mechanism can follow the processes describing in the figure 2.5

Figure 2.5 Linkage between academic researchers and firms with national funds

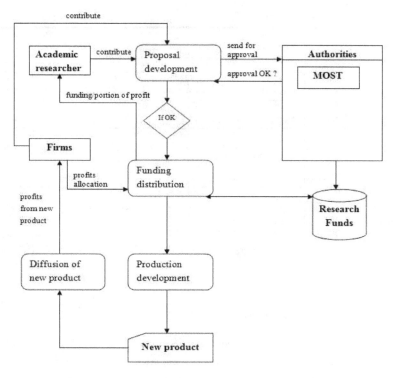

2.3.3.4 Idea implementation

In assessing the firm ability in turning new ideas into new products, this analysis looks at firm's experiences, the capacity of human resources and the financial capacity. For the firm experience, in the World Bank data set, the analysis looks at the international certification and the technology licensing. Table 2.7 provides that only 30.8% of firms own an international certification. However, the empirical result in table 2.8 suggests that firms having international certifications are significantly able to implement new ideas. Logically, this makes sense, because firms must proof to international organizations that they are satisfied the requirements ruled by the organizations prior to their certifications granted.

Table 2.7. Descriptive statistics for firms' ability in implementing new ideas

| | | | SURVEY DATA | | | | | | WORLD BANK DATA | | | |
| | | | size | | | | | | | size | | | |
			Small	Medium	Large	Total				Small	Medium	Large	Total
Firm ability to implement ideas													
Technology Licensing	0	Count	10	8	14	32	Technology Licensing	0	Count	350	70	46	466
		% of Total	15.6%	12.5%	21.9%	50.0%			% of Total	67.2%	13.4%	8.8%	89.4%
	1	Count	6	4	22	32		1	Count	32	12	11	55
		% of Total	9.4%	6.3%	34.4%	50.0%			% of Total	6.1%	2.3%	2.1%	10.6%
Patent Document	0	Count	16	10	23	49	International Certification	No	Count	308	32	20	360
		% of Total	25.0%	15.6%	35.9%	76.6%			% of Total	59.2%	6.2%	3.8%	69.2%
	1	Count	0	2	13	15		Yes	Count	73	50	37	160
		% of Total	.0%	3.1%	20.3%	23.4%			% of Total	14.0%	9.6%	7.1%	30.8%
							Employee Education	0	Count	353	76	52	481
Funding sources	0	Count	11	3	4	18			% of Total	68.0%	14.6%	10.0%	92.7%
		% of Total	17.2%	4.7%	6.3%	28.1%		1	Count	28	6	4	38
	1	Count	5	9	32	46			% of Total	5.4%	1.2%	.8%	7.3%
		% of Total	7.8%	14.1%	50.0%	71.9%	Training	0	Count	265	29	14	308
									% of Total	51.0%	5.6%	2.7%	59.2%
								1	Count	116	53	43	212
									% of Total	22.3%	10.2%	8.3%	40.8%

Source: own calculation based on World Bank (2009) and own survey

Table 2.7 also provides that only 10.6% of firms have acquired technology licensing. This figure is way smaller in comparison to firms in the dynamic group, where 50% of the firms expressed that they have acquired technology licensing. However, it is interesting to notice that a large percentage of firms purchase technology licensing does not necessarily means that the knowledge spillover would increase firms' ability in implementing ideas. Empirical evidence shows that Technology licensing is not significant to firms' innovation. This result may be supported by the finding of Álvarez et al. (2002) over the Chilean manufacturing firms. This indicates that the absorptive ability of Vietnamese firms is very weak. For the survey data, patent documents and technology licensing are important indicators for firms' ability in implementation of new ideas. Descriptive analysis provides that in the dynamic group, only 23.4% of the firms suggested that they have utilized the rich knowledge on the patent documents.

Table 2.8 Firm ability to implement ideas – Probit analysis

WORLD BANK DATA				SURVEY DATA			
Patent	Coef.	z	VIF	Patent	Coef.	z	VIF
Firm ability to implement ideas							
International Certification	0.519124	2.62***	1.21	Patent documents	1.54063	2.97**	1.19
Technology Licensing	-0.066	-0.24	1.07	Technology Licensing	0.16257	0.29	1.39
Employee Education	0.677284	2.55**	1.05	Employee Education	0.00511	0.45	1.37
Training	0.400783	2.02**	1.19	Funding sources	0.16658	0.24	1.28

Source: own calculation based on World Bank (2009) and own survey

** Significance at 95% level of confidence

*** Significance at 99% level of confidence

Empirical data provides that firms, which utilize more knowledge from patent documents, have better capacities in the process of implementation. In a similar assessment, empirical analysis does not find technology licensing significantly boost up firm's ability in implementing new ideas.

The World Bank data provides that firms are short for employees with higher education. Descriptive statistic suggests about 92.7% of firms short of employees with degrees. As for the World Bank data, the impacts of employees' education and training on the firm innovation are positively significant at 95% confidence. This suggests that education and training of employees are important factors to enhance and leverage employees' ability in the process of implementing new ideas. Despite of high propensity of HT&MH tech firms in the dynamic group, its employee education is not statistically significant. This suggests that the level of education supporting for the medium and high tech development is not satisfactory.

As funding makes the project spinning, so funding sources is critically importance for the implementation of new ideas and bring the outputs to markets. A majority of firms, especially the large firms in the survey agreed that funding source is important for the implementation. However, the empirical analysis suggests that the relationship between funding sources and firm's ability in implementation of new ideas is statistically insignificant. This suggests that firms are not able to access to the funding sources.

The institutional system of Vietnam should be a shame, when asking about their belief in the fairness of the court, about 65% of firms answered the question. Amongst them, only 3.3% of firms believed in the fairness of the court system (see table 2.9). This is a big challenge for the government to make changes to this judicial system. Empirical analysis suggests that the fairness of the court system is not statistical significance with the patent, although it poses a positive correlation. This means that the judicial system is not functioning to protect the right of the patent holder. This may discourage people to patenting.

Table 2.9 Ability to recognize barriers to innovation-Descriptive and Probit analysis

WORLD BANK DATA						WORLD BANK DATA		
		Size				Patent	Coef.	z
		Small	Medium	Large	Total	*Firm ability to recognize barriers to innovation*		
Ability to recognize barriers to innovation								
Court fairness	0 Count	246	55	25	326	Court fairness	0.20836	0.39
	% of Total	73.0%	16.3%	7.4%	96.7%			
	1 Count	10	0	1	11			
	% of	3.0%	.0%	.3%	3.3%			

Source: own calculation based on World Bank (2009) and own survey

Table 2.10 shows that only 6.3% of firms in the World Bank data set and only 14.1% of dynamic firms owning at least a patent in the past ten years makes the overall picture of firm innovativeness quite grey, although dynamic firms show a better innovative output. These figures indicate that the level of innovativeness of firms in Vietnam is quite low.

Table 2.10 Innovation output

			SURVEY DATA							WORLD BANK DATA			
			Size							Size			
			Small	Medium	Large	Total				Small	Medium	Large	Total
Firm characteristics													
Patent	0	Count	15	11	29	55	Patent	0	Count	365	73	50	488
		% of Total	23.4%	17.2%	45.3%	85.9%			% of Total	70.1%	14.0%	9.6%	93.7%
	1	Count	1	1	7	9		1	Count	17	9	7	33
		% of Total	1.6%	1.6%	10.9%	14.1%			% of Total	3.3%	1.7%	1.3%	6.3%

Source: own calculation based on World Bank (2009) and own survey

2.3.4 Multivariate analysis

In the previous section, each major competency has been assessed against patent, which plays as a proxy to measure firm innovation. Although, it is not reflected the true relationship between the firms' competencies and firms' innovation, it provides the magnitude of the influence of each of the competencies to the firms' innovation. As, firms utilize all of their competencies to make their operations spinning, this analysis considers the impacts of all of the firm's competencies to the firms' innovation's proxy. Table 2.11 provides that legal business types significantly indicate firms' innovation. Base on this empirical evidence, SOEs seem active in filing for patent protection. This does not mean that other firms (private and foreign) are passive in protecting their intellectual assets. It simply reflects that the protection mechanism has been very weak and there is not much benefit to filing for protection, as descriptive analysis provides that 96.7% of firms have lost their belief in the fairness of the court system. Furthermore, the empirical analysis also provides that employees' education is one of the critical factors that make firms growth, even though it is not a critical factor in the dynamic group. This confirms that the leverage of employees' education contribute to firm innovation. However, the insignificance of employees' education in the dynamic group may indicate that there is a problem with the quality of education. Additionally, the empirical results suggest that providing reward would create a better innovative performance of the employees within the firm.

Table 2.11 Multivariate analysis

WORLD BANK DATA			
Log likelihood = -61.152776	Number of obs =		333
	LR chi2(9) =		28.96
	Prob > chi2 =		0.0007
	Pseudo R2 =		0.1915
Patent	**Coef.**	**z**	**P>|z|**
Tech OECD	0.1886	0.54	0.588
Legal Business Type	0.3902	2.18**	0.029
Size	-0.1121	-0.49	0.626
Age	0.0118	1.41	0.157
International Certification	0.2766	0.95	0.341
Technology License	-0.0471	-0.13	0.898
Employees' education	0.8571	2.87***	0.004
Training	0.2419	0.88	0.377
Court fairness	0.568	1	0.319
_cons	-2.5889	-7.25	0
SURVEY DATA			
	Number of obs =		64
	LR chi2(13)=		24.54
	Prob > chi2=		0.0106
Log likelihood = -13.717799	Pseudo R2=		0.4722
patent	**Coef.**	**z**	**P>|z|**
Age	-0.03545	-1.4	0.163
Tech OECD	0.659701	0.88	0.378
Size	0.978863	1.42	0.157
Legal Business Type	0.089295	0.23	0.82
Innovation contest	0.226671	0.31	0.757
Reward	1.60525	2.25**	0.024
CT168 (program 168)	0.917202	1.36	0.174
Employee education	0.012667	0.68	0.494
Collaboration with external sources for ideas	1.342666	1.49	0.135
Technology License	0.084544	0.11	0.913
Funding Source	-0.20307	-0.15	0.878
_cons	-5.9964	-2.31	0.021

Source: own calculation based on World Bank (2009) and own survey
*** Significance at 95% level of confidence*

Although age does not significantly indicate firms' innovation, it is highly correlated. However, the positive correlation in the WBS and the negative correlation in the dynamic group suggest that in general older firms tend to be more innovative than younger firms, but in the dynamic group the relationship is reversed. This might be explained that the one that has survived through the "Doi Moi" and operate well in the market economy are in advantage for innovation. However, in the dynamic group, younger firms tend to explore and exploit new technology for their market entries that make them more innovative.

Other factors, such as: international certification, training, participation in the program 168, collaboration with external sources for ideas and fairness of the judgment are also very much correlated with firms' innovation, although they are not significant. These signals provide shading lights for authorities when assessing firms' innovation. Base on that, authorities, managers can laid out crucial policies that push firms forward.

2.4 Conclusion and Remarks

As Vietnam have been in the transitional phase from central planned economy to market economy, and most importantly private and foreign businesses have been legalized. This fundamental change not only provides opportunities for private firms and foreign firms, but it also forces SOE firms to change their behavior and the way of management in order to survive or to be privatized or dissolved. After almost two decades of reformation, the economy has experienced a rapid growth of private firms, a moderate growth of foreign firms, and a diminishment of SOEs. In such, economic circumstance, being able to identify innovative firms and recognize factors that influence firms' innovation would help authorities and board managements of firms to have suitable policies to make firms more productive.

In this transitional economy, where state still entirely operates firms or influences firms' execution (when state holds a larger share through privatization process), generally SOE firms are perceived to have more advantages over private firms and foreign firms. These advantages are reflected in the subsidies of information, funding resources and network. Although, SOEs firms are advantages, they have been transformed themselves significantly to avoid being dissolution or operating at loss. The output of the analysis show that SOEs firm is more innovative in the general group, but this is not confirmed in the dynamic group. Although, this creates suspicion on the sustainable innovative activities of

SOEs, it indicates that SOEs have been aware of the benefit of filing for protection of their intellectual assets.

Looking at the technological characteristic of firms, this analysis does not find MH &HT firms are more innovative than LT&ML firms. This not only suggests that the technological capacity of firms is very low, but it also urges the government provide crucial policies to build up high quality of human capital and provide an attractive business environment to encourage investors to invest in high tech areas.

In answering the second research question, this analysis found that some factors in the culture of innovation influence firms' innovativeness. Attractive incentive packages, such as reward and study opportunity, would positively reinforce employees' contribution to the development and growth of firms. So managers of firms should learn how to intelligently reward employees for their performances and provide employees with opportunities to acquire knowledge and skills for later contributions. Moreover, this study also looks into the aggressiveness of firms in acquiring knowledge on intellectual property. Interestingly, this analysis found that firms participate in the program 168 tend to be more innovative. This finding sounds logically, as innovative firms should find ways to protect their intellectual assets.

Further analysis confirms that firms' collaboration plays an important role in generating innovative outputs. Important determinants, such as supplier, customer, and university personnel are critical external sources for innovative ideas that lead to innovative outputs.

Most often, firms need to have personnel competence, technological competence, and financial competence to turn new ideas into new processes or products. In this research, personnel competence is measured by employees' educations and supportive training programs. In general, empirical data suggests that firms with higher average years of education are likely patented more. In the dynamic group, when firm innovation is measured by the percentage of employees holding degrees, empirical data provides that the relationship is insignificant. Furthermore, empirical evidences show that firms support training programs would likely patent more than the ones, which do not support. These results may suggest that employees' education is important for firms' innovation. However, employees might not absorb necessary knowledge and skills to work in high tech areas. In addition to that, empirical data suggests that firms, which are able to use patent documents, are more innovative. Indeed, patent document is considered very valuable source, which have been explored and exploited frequently by innovative firms in the world, but they have not been visible to major portion of firms in Vietnam. This indicates that either firms do not have sufficient quality human resources to explore this valuable source or it is not easy for firm to access to these documents.

As in the case of Vietnam, many firms have claimed that they often have to re-train their new recruited employees, who just graduated from the universities or colleges. Therefore, this finding supports these claims and urges the policy maker to find strategic ways to lift up the quality of education in Vietnam and bring it closer to the reality. Moreover, supporting policies should be introduced to encourage individuals and firms to access to patent documents. Knowledge spillover from patent documents not only brings new ideas but also assists firms in the implementation process.

Final implication, which is drawn from this finding, is the barrier to innovation. As a large proportion of firms do not believe in the fairness of the court system in Vietnam. Although, it is not significantly correlated, it is positively correlated. This leads to an indication that firms do not believe in the fairness judgment of the court, hence they find alternative ways to protect their intellectual assets.

Base on the above findings, this analysis suggest that (1) at macro level, two actions should be strategically implemented. The first one is the reformation of education system to bring its practices closer to the reality. The second one is a double action that not only requires the propagation of IPR knowledge, but it also demands a fairer judicial system. (2) At micro level, managers of firms should intelligently reinforce employees' positive behaviors with attractive packages. In building up employees' capacity, firms should provide trainings and select qualified employees through recruitment processes. Furthermore, managers should also encourage the R&D departments or R&D experts to look at different patent documents relating to firms' interest to get more valuable knowledge. Finally, firms should also find an appropriability regime to effectively protect their intellectual assets.

CHAPTER 3. AN INSIGHT INTO THE PATENT SYSTEMS OF FAST DEVELOPING ASEAN COUNTRIES

Objectives:

The first aim of this chapter is to describe the patent systems of fast developing ASEAN countries (Indonesia, Malaysia, Philippines, Singapore, Thailand and Vietnam) and China. Furthermore, it determines the factors that drive the demand for patents in these countries. Patent systems in these countries have now been strengthened to a large extent, the number of patent applications has increased drastically, although at a very different pace across countries. The policy features that seem to be associated with a strong increase in demand for patents are: i) policies aiming at attracting FDI; ii) low relative costs (or fees); and iii) a relatively low quality of the examination processes. The significant differences in the patent systems of fast developing countries echo the differences observed between the patent systems in Europe, the USA and Japan.

3.1 Introduction

Developing ASEAN countries and China have benefited from being amongst the top fast growing economies in the world for the past 15 years. They are viewed as promising markets for technology transfer and knowledge spillover in the world. At the same time their economies have evolved towards more openness. One aspect of this openness has been to gradually adapt their patent systems to world standards, essentially through their WTO membership. From 1991 to 2008, these countries saw a fast growing volume of patent applications. Yet there are important differences across countries. The objective of the present paper is to describe and compare these patent systems, and investigate the main drivers of the observed growth in patent applications of the countries under investigation comprising of China, Indonesia, Malaysia, Philippines, Singapore, Thailand and Vietnam.

Based on the literature, three factors are worth being considered: FDI policies, the cost of patenting and the quality of examination processes. These three factors have received attentions in the recent literature and this paper aims at investigating their role for the China and fast growing ASEAN countries. The paper is structured as follows.

Section 2 provides a broad picture of IPR systems in the seven countries. This comparative analysis illustrates similarities and differences across countries. Section 3 is devoted to the role of FDI and patent fee, which theoretically play a significant role in boosting growths of patent filings. Section 4 investigates the potential impact of the quality of the examination process on the demand for patents. Section 5 provides concluding remarks.

3.2 Overview of IPR system in fast developing ASEAN countries and China.

3.2.1 Historical development of IPR system in developing Asian countries

Historically, the Asian culture has not supported the principles of Intellectual Property Rights. In the past memorizing and imitating literature and paintings from well known masters were considered as the ways to show respects to those authors (Kumar and Ellingson, 2007). Secrecy was the most common way to keep ownership of process or product in the past. This argument can be seen clearly through the Traditional Asian Herbal Drugs; the secrecy of some medicines or methods were kept and only passed on to family's members. The eldest son normally was the one who received the secrecy and inherited the ownership. These practices can also be clearly seen in the wine industry and vocational villages.

The establishment of formal intellectual property systems in fast developing ASEAN countries is rather slow and embedded in more complex judicial systems. Except Singapore and Malaysia, their IP system had been relied on the Intellectual property office of UK for a long time even after their declarations of independence. For most of other countries, a formal intellectual property system was established a few years after their declarations of independence. However, it took many years for these IP systems to be enacted. They are designed by patent offices which were often first established as small units inside a ministry, such as ministry of trade or ministry of science and technology (see Table 3.1 for more details). Example, the patent office in Vietnam is one unit of the National Office of Intellectual Property (NOIP), which is managed by the Ministry of Science and Technology. The NOIP handles most of the categories relating to intellectual property, except for the copyright (handle by Ministry of Cultural, Tourism and Sports), and the Plant and Variety protection (handle by the Ministry of Agriculture and Urban Development).

Table 3.1 Patent offices and their competence administrations

Country	Patent Office	Administrative management
China	SIPO (State Administration for Intellectual Property Office of People's Republic of China)	State
Indonesia	DGIP (Directorate General of Intellectual Property)	Ministry of Laws and Human Rights
Malaysia	Intellectual Property Corporation of Malaysia (MyIPO)	Ministry of Domestic Trade, Co-operative and Consumerism
Philippines	IPOP (Intellectual Property Office of the Philippines)	Office of President
Singapore	IPOS (Intellectual Property Office of Singapore)	Ministry of Law
Thailand	DIP (Department of Intellectual Property)	Ministry of Commerce
Vietnam	NOIP (National Office of Intellectual Property)	Ministry of Science and Technology

Source: WIPO website http://www.wipo.int/members/en/index.jsp

3.2.2 IPR enforcement and patent protection

The seven countries under investigation have fairly new intellectual property laws. Except Malaysia and Singapore, IP enforcement processes of the other countries are however considered very weak and embodied with a high degree of uncertainty. Most of infringement cases were administratively solved, less than 1% of the cases were turned over for prosecution.

Based on the evaluation of the United States Trade Representative (USTR) on the seriousness of IPR's violation, in 2010 special 301 report[8] (USTR, 2010), USTR placed Indonesia and Thailand in the priority watch list and the Philippines, Malaysia and Vietnam in the watch list. Additionally, table 3.2 shows the estimations performed by Business Software Alliance (2010) for the seven countries over the period of 2005-2009. It clearly appears that software piracy rates have slightly declined in the seven countries, but their rates are still very high, except Singapore. The values of pirated software have however increased.

Table 3.2 Business Software Alliance estimation on pirated software.

Country	Percentage of Pirated Software					Value of Pirated Software $ Million				
	2005	2006	2007	2008	2009	2005	2006	2007	2008	2009
China	86	82	82	80	79	3,884	5,429	6,664	6,677	7,583
Indonesia	87	85	84	85	86	280	350	411	544	886
Malaysia	60	60	59	59	58	149	289	311	368	453
Philippines	71	71	69	69	69	76	119	147	202	217
Singapore	40	39	37	36	35	86	125	159	163	197
Thailand	80	80	78	76	75	259	421	468	609	694
Vietnam	90	88	85	85	85	38	96	200	257	353

Source: Business Software Alliance (2010)

---

[8] The USTR annually produces a special 301 report, which provides information on the administration's effort in handling IPR protection worldwide. Detailed reports could be found at http://www.ustr.gov

In an evaluation for intellectual property protection for the year 2010, the World economics forum (WEF) ranked these countries over 139 evaluated countries in the world (see table 3.3 for details). Except Singapore, these ranks reflect well the fact that the IP enforcement systems of the remaining countries have not yet been completed and there have been a shortage of well trained IP personnel for IP registration office, judicial system, and enforcement system.

Table 3.3 WEF – IP protection ranking for the year 2010

Country	IP Protection ranking over 139 countries
Singapore	3
Malaysia	33
China	49
Indonesia	58
Thailand	84
Philippines	103
Vietnam	109

Source: WEF(2010)

Ginarte and Park (1997) provided an alternative way to assess the strength of IPR systems, including enforcements practices (preliminary injunction, contributory infringement and burden of proof reversal). These criterions are somewhat legitimate but they do not take into account the effective implementation of these regulations. In order to have a better view on enforcement systems two extra criterions are added to the three factors taken into account by Park (2008): the existence of an IP court and the observed level of copyrights violations. The broad evaluation IPR enforcement system is therefore based on the 5 criteria presented in table 3.4 (preliminary injunction; contributory infringement; burden of proof reversal; having a specialized IP court; moderate violation in copyrights). Each criterion is given 0.2 point when fulfilled. For the violation of copyrights, a threshold value of 50% is chosen to identify the countries with a low effective enforcement. The evaluation of enforcement practices for the seven countries is presented in table 3.4.

Table 3.4 IPR enforcement systems in the seven Asian countries for the year 2009

Enforcement norm	China	Indonesia	Malaysia	Philippines	Singapore	Thailand	Vietnam
Preliminary Injunction	0.2	0.2	0.2	0.2	0.2	0.2	0.2
Contributory Infringement	0.2			0.2			
Burden of Proof Reversal	0.2	0.2	0.2	0.2	0.2	0.2	0.2
Existence of an IP Court	0.2		0.2		0.2	0.2	
Moderate violation in copyrights *					0.2		
Enforcement Index	**0.8**	**0.4**	**0.6**	**0.6**	**0.8**	**0.6**	**0.4**

Source: adopted from Ginarte & Park (1997)

* Moderate violation in copyright of each country is evaluated base on the percentage of pirated software, which is presented in Table 2.

Preliminary injunction is available in the seven countries. However, its implementation varies in practices. For example, even though preliminary injunction is applicable in Vietnam, it is not clearly introduced in the IPR law. Furthermore, the court only issues preliminary injunction if the claimant has paid a deposit, which should be equal to 20% of the value of the suspected infringed goods (Joint circular No.2/2008). Perceptions on IP enforcement vary as well in the ways of prosecution. Some countries consider IP infringement as a criminal activity, like in Thailand, whereas other countries, like in Vietnam and China frequently consider it as an administrative matter. The perception also depends on types of infringement. Sorg (2009) provided evidences that most of the infringement cases relating to copyright and trademark in Thailand were criminally proceeded, whereas the infringement cases relating to inventions or industrial designs were rarely proceeded with for criminal prosecution.

As summarized in Table 3.5, we notice that all these countries follow the first to file scheme, which is different with the first to invent of US patent system. These systems share many characteristics in common, such as: the maximum duration of patent protection, which is 20 years without possibility of extension; the grace period is 6 months for Indonesia, Thailand and Vietnam and 12 months for Malaysia, the Philippines and Singapore. The procedure of patenting is varied from country to country, but in general, it follows the first to file principle: filing, preliminary examination, publication, substantive examination, and granting or refusal. Most of these countries allow pre-grant opposition (except Singapore).

Table 3.5 Comparison of patent systems in ASEAN countries, China and the USA in the year 2009.

Country	Patent System Scheme	Grace Period	Publication	Opposition	Request for examination from filing date	Duration of Protection
China	First to file	6 months	18 months	No	36 months	20 years
Indonesia	First to file	6 months	18 months	Pregrant[a]	36 months	20 years
Malaysia	First to file	12 months	18 months	Pregrant	24 months	20 years
Philippines	First to file	12 months	18 months[b]	Pregrant	24 months	20 years
Singapore	First to file	12 months	18 months	Postgrant	21 months[c] or 39 months[d]	20 years
Thailand	First to file	6 months	not specified	Pregrant	60 months[e]	20 years
Vietnam	First to file	6 months	18 months	Pregrant	42 months	20 years
USA	First to invent	12 months	18 months	No	-	20 years

Source: WIPO http://www.wipo.int/members/en/index.jsp and WTO http://docsonline.wto.org/

a: Opposition must be made within 6 months of the publication date.
b: Publication must be made within 12 to18 months of the filing date.
c: Fast track
d: Slow track
e: Request for examination must be made within 90 days from the publication date.

All countries allow owners of inventions to file patents by themselves, however it is recommended to consult with IP law firms or IP experts to draft the patent application. Non resident applicants need to have a local IP firm acting as a representative to file for a patent. All the studied countries allow certain time frames (grace periods) prior to the filing date for the inventions being considered as novelty.

3.3 The demand for patents

The objective of this paper is to identify the factors that might influence the demand for patents in fast developing ASEAN countries. It is therefore useful to have a glance through their patent systems. Realizing on the works of Ford and Rork (2010), Pavitt (1985), and recent studies by de Rassenfosse and van Pottelsberghe (2010), (2011), the two factors (Inward FDI and Patenting fee) are analyzed in this section.

3.3.1 FDIs and patent filings

Three patent intensity indicators can be used to assess the development of IPR system: resident patent filings per US$ billion gross domestic product; resident patent filings per million capita; Resident patent filings per US$ million of research and development (R&D) expenditure. Hu and Jefferson (2009) suggest that FDI create patenting opportunities in China and hence contribute to increase the demand for patents. Ford and Rock (2010) illustrates the positive correlation between FDI and resident patenting for the US. Nunnenkamp and Spatz (2004) provide empirical evidence suggesting that stronger IPR protection may induce better quality FDI, thus ultimately increasing patents both in volume and in quality. As the principle of IPR protection is to motivate institution to invent and innovate, through a reduction of infringements, stronger of IPR systems should result in a higher demand, notably via higher FDI.

Based on the above empirical studies, we can present the relationship between Resident patent filings and FDI in the following function:

Resident Patent$_i$ = f (FDI$_i$)

where i presents the year in the period of 1991-2008.

Table 3.6 provides the two variables: Resident Patent and FDI, which are significantly correlated. Its coefficient is significant at the 0.01 level (2 tailed). This finding is consistent with the empirical findings mentioned above. Therefore, FDI induces the growth of resident patent in the seven countries.

Table 3.6 Correlation between FDI and Resident patent filing in period of 1991-2008

		Resident Patent	FDI
Resident Patent	Pearson Correlation	1	.868**
	Sig. (2-tailed)		.000
	N	126	120

Source: own calculation with the usage of data collected from WIPO, SIPO;DGIP; MYIPO; IPOP; IPOS; DIP; NOIP and UNCTAD.

** Correlation is significant at the 0.01 level (2-tailed).

The significant correlation also suggests that FDI contributed to the growth of technological capability, and stimulated the demand for patents in all studying countries. The size of each market for patents in these countries can be seen through their motivation to patenting. Reviewing the number of patent applications received by the patent offices in the seven countries for the period of 1990-2008, important increases in the numbers of resident patent filings (see Appendix 2) clearly appear. The motivation to patent can be assessed through patent intensity, which is shown in table 3.7.

Table 3.7 Average resident patent intensity[9] over 5 year periods

Period	1991-1995	1996-2000	2001-2005	2006-2008
China	8.5	12.7	44.4	119.4
Indonesia	0.2	0.5	1.0	1.3
Malaysia	8.8	9.2	16.2	25.9
Philippines	2.3	1.9	1.8	2.4
Singapore		87.7	143.0	152.6
Thailand	1.9	7.3	11.5	14.2
Vietnam	0.4	0.4	1.2	2.4
US	393	488	653	768

Source: Own calculation based on data collected from WIPO (see Appendix 2) and World Bank.

The big differences in amounts of FDI per million capita and patent intensity reflect the transparence of the economy, the economic policy, and technological capability of each of the country in general. Malaysia and Singapore are the two commonwealth countries, which have been influenced very much by the UK's economic system. Many of their business services have been stemming from the UK. For example: intellectual property registration activities had been done by the Intellectual property Office of the UK for both Malaysia and Singapore. Singapore is geographically considered to be in a good location. Even though, it has a little natural resource, the economy was ranked number 3 in the world for global competitive index in 2010 (WEF, 2010). Having the highest patent intensity amongst the seven countries, Singapore is considered as the most advanced technology country in this group. Moreover, it has created a sound business environment to attract foreign investments, leading to more than 7,000 multinational firms coming from US and EU to operate their businesses in Singapore.

China has been perceived in the last decade for the advancement in science

---

[9] Average resident patent intensity = Resident patent filings / Million capita (Calculation is based on 5 year period)

and technology. Prior to 2005, the technology advancement of China was far behind the Singapore that was reflected through much lower patent intensity. However, the growth of Science and Technology of China has been impressively. If China maintains this speed of development, it will catch up Singapore in the period 2015-2020.

Malaysia is considered as the third attractive market for patenting. However, not only its patent intensity is much far behind its neighboring country (Singapore), but its FDI per million capita is only accounted for less than 10 percents of the amount being observed in Singapore. This suggests that the market for patenting in Malaysia is less attractive than Singapore.

Being endowed with an educated workforce and having developed policies designed to attract FDI, including a strong IPR judicial system, the Thai government has succeeded in attracting large amounts of foreign investments, even more than China in relative terms. It received $2 billion of FDI in 1991, and nearly five fold this amount in 2008. Open policies to foreign investors and the strengthening of its IPR enforcement system made the Thai patent market become more attractive, and became the third largest market for patenting amongst the six ASEAN countries.

Vietnam, the Philippines and Indonesia are now having quite similar market size for patenting, though these markets are quite small in comparison to the ones of Singapore and Malaysia or even Thailand. To get to this state Vietnam has opened its door for foreign investments since the early 1990s. Numbers of incentive policies have been implemented including tax reduction, usage of land, and administrative procedures. Incentive policies and competitive labor costs have attracted considerable amounts of investments from Japan, South Korea, US and EU. In 1991, Vietnam attracted only $375 million of FDI, but this amount has been grew up to $8 billion in 2008.

Witnessing the raise in FDI, NOIP has also experienced growths in patent applications filing from both resident and non resident applicants. Statistical data shows that in 1991, NOIP received 72 patent applications (37 resident patent applications and 35 non resident patent applications). By 2008, NOIP received a total of 3,199 patent applications, which mainly were filed from non-resident applicants (204 resident patent applications, 2,995 non resident patent applications). These figures mean that even though, Vietnam succeeded in attracting more and more FDIs, and these FDIs had contributed to raise the technological capacity of Vietnam through out the period. However, the technological capacity of Vietnam is still marginal compared to Singapore, Malaysia and Thailand. Number of patents filed per million capita in 2008 was about the same as number of patents per million capita of Thailand filed in 1991. Moreover, numbers of resident patent applications were very small in comparison to numbers of foreign patent applications received over the period. This suggests that Vietnam has devoted more efforts to attract FDI rather than strengthen its internal technological capability.

In the early 1990s, Indonesia attracted much more FDI than Vietnam. The period of 1991-1996, the amount of FDI was increased from 1.5 billions to over 6.2 billions. Patent filings also increased from 1,314 filings in 1991 to 4,067 in 1996. Affecting from both of the Asian financial crisis and political crisis, the amount of FDI was radically decreased, thus many foreign investments were pulled out in the period of 1997 to 2003, resulted in negative inflow of FDI. Non resident patent filings were also free-felled in 1998 but then gained its momentum to rise back again. In different view, resident patent filings were steadily increased, even though at small margins. Table 3.7 shows that Indonesia weakly improved its technological capacity and its patent market is even less attractive than the market of the Philippines and Vietnam.

Table 3.7 shows that the technological capacity of the Philippines has actually almost stepped still. This might due to the fact that the Philippines has not been aggressive enough to provide incentive policies in attracting foreign investments. In 1991 the Philippines received only $556 million, which is about one and half of the FDI, which was poured into Vietnam for the same year. However, by the year 1994, the amount of FDI, which was poured into Vietnam, was over taken the amount, which was received by the Philippines. Moreover, political uncertainties and frequent foreign investment disputes has created unfavorable conditions for foreign investors, leading to the amount of FDI went up and down through out the period.

Based on the patent intensity (numbers of total patents per million capita), the FDI (million dollar per million inhabitants), and the correlation between the FDI and patent applications, Table 3.8 provides a quick assessment on the attractiveness of the seven countries. Singapore, China, Malaysia and Thailand are the four most attractive countries for patenting, though the attractive gaps are quite wide. Vietnam and the

Philippines will have a hard time to catching up Thailand, Malaysia, China and then Singapore. Indonesia is being the least attractive country for patenting.

Table 3.8 Quick assessment of the attractiveness of patent market for the seven Asian countries for the year 2008.

Country	Patent intensity	FDI per million capita	Level of Attractiveness
Singapore	2019.2	1,717.6	1
China	220	82.2	2
Malaysia	200.1	265.6	3
Thailand	101.8	152.9	4
Vietnam	36.5	91.5	5
Philippines	34.5	15.8	6
Indonesia	21.6	33.3	7

Source: data derived from UNCTAD (2010), World Bank (2010) and WIPO (2010)

3.3.2 Patent Costs

Patenting fee schedules are heterogeneous and complex. The cost of patenting is essentially driven by the patenting strategy adopted by the firm (geographical scope, quality of drafting, number of claims, and number of pages). Patent costs can be measured through simulations, as evidenced in van Pottelsberghe and François (2009) and van Pottelsberghe and Mejer (2010) for large patent systems. De Rassenfosse and van Pottelsberghe (2010) provide an in-depth analysis of the role of fees in patent systems and compare a large number of countries. The costs associated with one patent increase over time, and must therefore be assessed through a cumulative approach. Van Pottelsberghe and François (2009) rely on the following structure of fees (these costs do not including the drafting costs and the search for prior art by the patent attorney):

- The filing of a patent

- Searching for prior art by the patent office (and search report)

- Patent publication (after 18 months)

- Substantive examination

- Grant, Refusal or withdrawal

- Possibility of appeal and opposition process

The authors then break down the cost of patenting into four major categories (process costs; translation costs; external expenses; maintenance costs):

Process cost is made up of the total fees for filing, publication, search, examination and granting a patent application. These fees are differed from one country to another country, from one region to another region. For the five Asian countries, their patent offices are governmental units, and the fees are set by the governments. Patent applicants can be residents of their own country or can be residents of other countries (non residents). The cost of filing presented in this paper is the direct filing by domestic applicants. Table 3.9 presents the detail fees for the seven countries.

External expense is the sum of incurred costs, which are paid to a third party (often an IP law firm) for drafting services and interaction with the patent office. Even through these services often are not mandated by laws, they are highly recommended. The variations in fees and quality of services of the patent law firms make the calculation of the external expenses very complex and not straight forward. Due to the unavailable reliable data sources for external expenses, this paper will take service fees providing by a private IP law firm in each of the countries to serve as external expenses for that country.

Maintenance cost is the total renewal fees needed to keep a patent in force for a certain period up to 20 years in the total life of the patent. Some countries require the patentee to pay for the renewal fee each year or in period.

The cost of patenting depends to a significant extent on the number of pages and the number of claims included in the patent. Since there is no reliable data on the average number claims and average number of pages as well as average number of figures in a patent application for these countries. By interviewing different patent experts in the NOIP and INVENCO[10] about the claims, pages and figures in a patent application, on average a patent application contains about 10 claims, 30 pages and 7 figures. These figures will be used as a building block for our cost simulations. All the cost figures is measured by the international dollar with the conversion rate of the

---

[10] INVENCO is a patent law firm, which receives about 30% of the total patent application of Vietnamese market.

year 2008.

Based on our assumptions, Vietnam has similar filing cost figures as Indonesia and the Philippines. However, it can be very expensive if patentees have more claims in their patent applications, since the fee for patenting is claim dependent. The fee can also be topped up for each page exceeding 5 pages or exceeding one drawing. With the suggested assumption, the official patenting fee (without attorney's fees) is approximately $587 for a patent application filing in Vietnam. Although, it is not compulsory for residents of Vietnam to acquire services from an IP law firm, it is recommended for them to do so. Non resident applicants must use an IP law firm as their representatives. Based on the above assumption, the patenting costs including external fees for resident applicant and non resident applicant are to be $1,186.5 and $3,386.5 respectively. Because of the translation cost adding up, the cost for non resident patent applicant is almost three times higher in comparison to the patenting cost of resident applicant. Additionally, the cost to maintain a patent in force for 10 years is $1,202 and for 20 years is $5,853 (for details, see Table 3.9).

Indonesia also has a claim-based fee system, where applicant has to pay additional fee for the 11th claim onward. The cumulated official fee for a patent application is approximately $978. In a similar patenting policy with Vietnam, external service fees are only applied to non resident applicants. So, the cost of patenting with the usage of external service is to be $1,978.5 for resident applicant and $6,978.5 for non resident patent applicant. Once a patent is registered, the fee to maintain the patent in force increases drastically from the fifth year to year ten. However, it is fixed from the year 11th onward. The cost to maintain a patent in force for 10 years is around $2,867 and for 20 years is $12,054.

Thailand on the other hand requests a fixed amount for a patent application regardless of the number of pages or claims. The cost to obtain a patent for an invention in Thailand is approximately $120, which is the lowest among the five countries. External services of an IP law firm are optional to resident applicant, though they are compulsory to non resident applicant. In usage of these services, the patenting cost for resident patent applicant and non resident patent applicant is to be $950.3 and $3,450.3 respectively. The cost to maintain a patent in force for 10 years is approximately $2,527 and for 20 years is around $26,469, which is the most expensive among the five countries. Applicant can get a discount of around $2,400 if they agree to pay upfront for the entire 20 years of protection.

The Philippines also have claim-based and page-based fee schedules. Additional fees are required if the application contains more than 5 claims or 30 pages. The Philippines gives incentives to "Small" entities and young inventors to patent for their inventions by reducing approximately 50% of the patenting fees. Table 3.9 shows the full patenting fee for "Big" entity, which is around $606. So the patenting cost for a "Small" entity should be around $300. Since, the Philippines uses English as its official language, no translation is required if the patent application is in English. The cost for patenting for resident and non resident is the same, and equal to $1,156.1. The cost to maintain the protection for 10 years is $1,478 and 20 years is $13,814.

As the cost figure presents, China follows claim-based fee schedules. Calculation of the patenting cost can be quite complicated. Patent application has more than 30 pages is required to pay extra fee per additional page. This fee is even more expensive for application with 100 pages or over. In the same philosophy with most of the country, Chinese government and other governments would encourage patent holders to surrender their patents to public by increase rapidly the renewal fees to maintain their patents in force. As the table 3.9 provides the cost up to grant is about $2,177 and the total cost to keep the patent in force for 10 years (cost to grant plus renewal fees) is about $5,636. However, the total cost for 20 years is nearly 4 folds of the total cost to keep the patent in force for 10 years.

Singapore and Malaysia also apply claim bases fee schedules in calculating cost for patenting. Since English is their official language, so there is no need for translation if patent application was already written in English. Singapore is different with other countries, since it out sources external patent offices to do search and substantive examination for its patent applications. Therefore, the cost for patenting in Singapore is quite expensive. The cost up to grant is about $2,731, which is the most expensive amongst the seven countries. Usage of services of an IP law firm is optional. However, if one would like to use this kind of service, the patenting cost up to grant is expected around $9,031. Although it is expensive to file for a grant, once the patent is granted, the cost to maintain the patent in force in Singapore is considered much cheaper than other countries. In comparison to Singapore, the patenting cost for Malaysia is cheaper (details can be seen in the table 3.9)

Table 3.9 Patenting costs (National currencies & USPPP) for China, Indonesia, Malaysia, Philippines, Singapore, Thailand, and Vietnam in 2008.

Country	China	Indonesia	Malaysia	Philippines	Singapore	Thailand	Vietnam
Currency	Yuan	Rupiah	Ringgit	Peso	Dollar	Baht	Dong
Procedural fees							
Filing	950	575,000	290	3,600	160	1,000	1,500,000
Exceeding page				-			250,000
Exceeding claim		-		1,500			
Exceeding drawing							
Publication		250,000		5,550		500	100,000
Publication with drawings							300,000
Search	2,100	2,500,000					1,000,000
Examination	2,500	2,000,000	1,100	3,500	2,600^a		350,000
Granting	255				200	500	100,000
Administrative cost							
Registration fee/Printing/Stamp	255						-
Total procedure fees (Local currency)	**6,060**	**5,325,000**	**1,390**	**14,150**	**2,960**	**2,000**	**3,600,000**
Total procedure fees (US-PPP-2008)	**1,537**	**978**	**725**	**606**	**2,731**	**120**	**587**
External fee (counseling by IP firm)- USPPP-2008)	640	1000^b	2500^c	550^d	6,300^e	830^f	600^g
Total cost up to grant (Resident applicant)- USPPP-2008	**2177**	**1,979**	**3,225**	**1,156**	**9,031**	**950**	**1,187**
Maintain cost for 10 years (Local currency)	13,633	15,600,000	5,030	34,500	1,290	42,000	7,375,000
Maintain cost for 10 years (US-PPP-2008)	**3458**	**2,867**	**2,623**	**1,478**	**1,190**	**2,527**	**1,202**
Maintain cost for 20 years (Local currency)	82,300	65,600,000	16,490	322,500	4,700	440,000	35,925,000
Maintain cost for 20 years (US-PPP-2008)	**20,878**	**12,054**	**8,597**	**13,814**	**4,336**	**26,469**	**5,853**
Total cost for 10 years (Resident applicant)	**5,636**	**4,846**	**5,848**	**2,634**	**10,221**	**3,477**	**2,389**
Total cost for 20 years (Resident applicant)	**23,055**	**14,033**	**11,822**	**14,970**	**13,367**	**27,419**	**7,040**

Source: Data was calculated based on the patenting fee obtained from patent offices (see Appendix 3 for details) of presented countries with an assumption on a patent application, which averagely contains 10 claims, 30 pages, and 7 drawings.

    a: combination fee for search and examination
    b: provided by Shuba (IP law firm in Indonesia)
    c: provided by SKRINE (Malaysia)
    d: provided by The Office of Bagay-Villamor & Fabiosa (The Philippines)
    e: provided by Amica Law LLC (Singapore)
    f: provided by Tilleke & Gibbins International Ltd. (Thailand)
    g: provided by INVENCO (Vietnam)

Table 3.10 provides a comparison the USPTO patenting costs expressed in US PPPs (purchasing power parities), as computed by van Pottelsberghe and Mejer (2010). In the seven countries, except Singapore, Malaysia and China the cost of patenting up to the grant for resident patent application is much cheaper than in the US. Van Pottelsberghe (2011) suggests that low fees might be associated with a low quality of the examination process. Therefore, the quality of granted patent in those ASEAN countries will be analyzed in the next section. The maintenance costs over 10 years in most countries are however more expensive than in the US, that may imply that these countries' policies are encouraging inventors to try to protect their inventions. However, if a patent is effectively exploited, its cost logically increases, faster than in the US.

Table 3.10 Comparison of patenting costs and maintenance costs for resident applicants of the seven Asian countries with the US in the year 2008.

Country	China	Indonesia	Malaysia	Philippines	Singapore	Thailand	Vietnam	US
Total filing fee up to grant	**2,177**	**1,978**	**3,225**	**1,156**	**9,031**	**950**	**1,187**	**2,620**
Maintenance cost for 10 years	*3,458*	*2,867*	*2,623*	*1,478*	*1,190*	*2,527*	*1,202*	*3,290*
Total cost for 10 years	**5,636**	**4,846**	**5,848**	**2,634**	**10,221**	**3,477**	**2,389**	**5,910**
Maintenance cost for 20 years	*20,878*	*12,054*	*8,597*	*13,814*	*4,336*	*26,469*	*5,853*	*7,200*
Total cost for 20 years	**23,055**	**14,033**	**11,822**	**14,970**	**13,367**	**27,419**	**7,040**	**9,820**

Source: own calculation derived from IMF database and Appendix 3. The unit is measured in US PPP conversion rates for 2008.

Figure 3.1 shows a non linear relationship between the number of patents filed per million capita and the resident patenting cost over GDP per capita for the six ASEAN countries. A traditional non linear demand curve appears where Singapore has the highest relative demand for patents and the low relative value of cost over GDP per capita. Vietnam and Philippines has quite small number of patents per million capita and the moderate relative value of costs over GDP per capita. Indonesia has the least number of patents per million capita and the highest value of cost over GDP per capita. This might suggest that the more expensive (relative value of cost over GDP per capita) of the patenting process the less demand for patent protection.

Figure 3.1 Patent costs and demand for patents

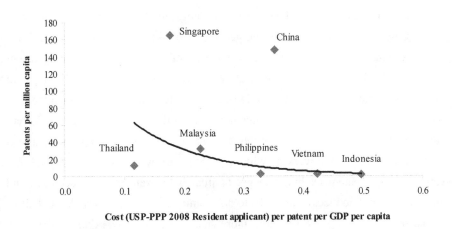

Cost (USP-PPP 2008 Resident applicant) per patent per GDP per capita

Source: Own calculation based on data of WIPO, IMF, World Bank and National patent fee scheme

3.4 Quality: patent examiners' skills and workload

Many research papers have pointed the negative consequences of granting low quality patents, such as: discouraging inventors, baring entries for small firms, slowing down the diffusion of technologies, increasing the litigations, discouraging spillover of knowledge and social interests (Hall et al., 2004). Patent quality is not straight forward to measure. There are numbers of factors influence to the quality of the granted patent quality, including "exhaustiveness of search and depth of examination" (Guellec and van Pottelsberghe, 2007). Van Pottelsberghe (2011) studied in details the many factors that might influence the quality of examination processes in three large patent offices (USPTO; JPO; EPO).

Overloaded examiners might reduce the quality of examination services. Quality also depends on the skills and experience of patent examiners and on the available infrastructure (working condition, search tools …etc.). Building and developing pool of human resources to allow for a sustainable quality of examination is highly demanded in these countries. Figure 3.2 shows that Chinese and Thai patent examiners have a much higher workload per head than in the four other countries. Govindaraju and Wong (2011) mentioned that Malaysia had been short of patent examiners, and it had led to serious backlogs in processing patent applications. Vietnam has a low average in patent granting rate. As in 2008, there were only 19% of resident patent filings that were granted, against 21% of non-resident patent filings.

Collectiveness of educations, formal trainings, on the job trainings, and years of experience in the field underlie the generation of skills and competencies. Most patent examiners in the studying countries are not formally trained to be patent examiners. As in Vietnam, the general requirement for a person to be a patent examiner is to have a bachelor degree in science and technology, and passed a public servant entry test[11]. There is no requirement for working experiences. Most patent examiners built up their skills through informal on the job training, international seminars, workshops, and working with peers. Statistically it would take about 3 to 5 years for a new patent examiner to get familiar with examination procedures and gather necessary knowledge and skills to do examination on their own. About half of the patent examiners at NOIP have more than 5 years of working experiences. Singapore, Malaysia, the Philippines, Thailand, and Indonesia have established their formal IP training systems at university levels for a couple of decades. Vietnam, however, still struggles to build curriculums for IP training. Most of the IP relating courses are about the basics of IP law, and often it is only accounted as a small unit in the whole four year degree program. The only place, where people can get deeper knowledge about IP is the NOIP's training centre, which provides training for professional certifications. However, the training capacity of the NOIP's training center is considered weak due to lack of lecturer, poor infrastructure, and lack of systemic curriculum.

Indonesia, the Philippines and Thailand are in a somewhat better position in approaching to intellectual property. Kariodimedjo (2006) shows that there are about 10 universities in Indonesia having curriculums relating to the training of IP, and few other universities and institutions were in processing of developing curriculums for

---

[11] A general test, which is applicable to everyone, who would like to serve in a public organization.

their trainings. The curriculums have been developed and the trainings were carried out for number of years. However, the author also indirectly mentioned that they were short of trainer and lecturers.

Except Singapore, most of the patent systems, which are analyzed in this paper, are generally considered of having poor working conditions and institutional infrastructures for their patent examiners. Lack of infrastructure, equipments, database and assessing to professional information create barriers to provide timely and better quality of examination (Drahos, 2008). Working condition is like a thorn in one eyes, however it is not easy to solve, since most of the studying countries are developing countries. Taking Vietnam is one of examples, the working condition at NOIP is considered as poor, even though it has been leveraged drastically in the past few years. A new entry patent examiner receives the same base salary as other public servant staff, which is normally about 1.9 million VND[12], which is about nearly 100USD per month. 10 years of working as a patent examiner, one would expect to receive 2.5 million VND (125 USD) per month, whereas a new graduate student working in a bank can receive a salary of 3 million VND and shortly can receive 5 million VND per month. In such situation, the NOIP applies the financial strategy of a public organization having revenue. So a small fixed amount is adding up the base salary of every one according to the seniority and management position. Furthermore, additional compensation can be attributed to patent examiners who perform more examination than scheduled. This would create incentives to patent examiners, however its economical reasons may also encourage patent examiners go for quantity rather than focus on improving quality of patent examination.

A correlation between costs of patenting with quality of patents granted was either directly or indirectly mentioned by MacLeod et al. (2003), Nicholas (2011) and van Pottelsberghe (2011). This induces that more expensive patenting cost leads to better quality of patent. Figure 3.2 shows a relationship between patents per examiner and official patenting fee up to grant per GDP per capita for presented countries in the year 2008. The curve shows that the cheaper of the official patenting fee per GDP per capita the higher is the workload per patent examiner.

---

[12] The salary is calculated by Salary rank * Minimum wage, leading to:
2.67 * 730,000VND= 1,941000 VND.

Figure 3.2 Official patenting fee-quality curve

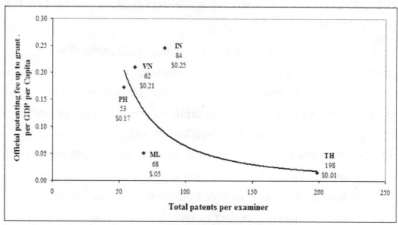

Source: Own calculation; data collected from WIPO, World Bank and National Patent Offices
Cost are measured in US-PPP at 2008 conversion rates
IN: Indonesia; ML: Malaysia; PH: Philippines; TH: Thailand; VN: Vietnam

3.5 Concluding remarks

This chapter has briefly described IPR systems in China, Indonesia, Malaysia, the Philippines, Singapore, Thailand and Vietnam. Overall, the IPR systems in these countries have improved, but low prosecution rates of infringements opposed to high rates of infringements suggests that their enforcement of patent rights were still considered weak and inefficient. By assessing their enforcement systems amongst the seven countries following the approach of Ginarte and Park (1997), this paper found that Singapore and China had the strongest IPR system, whereas Malaysia, Thailand and the Philippines had moderate IPR systems. Although, Indonesia and Vietnam were in the weakest group, there have been improvements in their system.

By looking at the FDI, patent intensities of those countries, this paper found that Singapore, China, Malaysia and Thailand are the three biggest markets for patenting. Providing favorable policies to attract FDI over the survey period, those countries have not only benefited from knowledge spill over, but also pushed innovators to file for patents.

Given assumptions on number of pages, number of claims, and number of drawings, a scenario of patent cost was constructed based on the official fees assigned by each of the presented countries' authorities. A non linear traditional demand curve was observed in studying the relationship between the cost per resident patent over GDP per capita and the patent per million capita. This suggests that cheaper patenting cost attracts more patent applications. This study also found that except Singapore, the cost schedules of the other presented countries do not support big patent application (many pages, many claims) and long protection.

Having cheaper costs up to grant for a patent, and being fast developing countries with attractive policies to attract FDI, these countries may experience backlog problems. This fast rate of growth of patent filings may become a heavy burden to their IP systems, which were assessed to have poor working conditions, informal training, and lack of experienced patent examiners. This induces doubts on the quality of granted patents.

These findings suggest authorities need to provide stronger actions on enforcement, and need to use the level of patent fees as an adjustment tool to balance the patent filings and workload of patent examiners, to ensure the quality of the patents granted. Working conditions, formal training, access to international patent databases and professional groups are necessities for patent examiners to improve the quality of their work.

CHAPTER 4. IPR ENFORCEMENT AND CASE STUDY

Objective

Increment in subjectivities and scope of protections over the last decade has proved that the system of IP and IPRs of Vietnam has been strengthened. A comparison of IP law between Vietnam, France, and the US on the mechanism of handling infringements provide a better judgment for the strengths and weaknesses of the IPR enforcement in Vietnam. This provides opportunities to compare two different systems (Vietnam and France) of civil law, to US common law. Handling IPRs infringement has been challenging for Vietnam due to the lack of IP knowledge and well trained staff. Among few strategies, which have been exercised, administrative procedure has been utilized very often. Although, the application of administrative measure does not create wide effect and strong enforcement, it is quick and produces immediate effect. Learning from selected case studies, this paper confirmed that administrative procedure is the preferable method in handling IP infringement in Vietnam. Given the fact that judicial procedure creates wider effects and stronger enforcement, it takes much longer time, and more costly. Base on these findings, this paper advises the government continue to improve the application of administrative procedure while promulgating IP and IPRs knowledge widely. In a longer term, the government should provide systematic trainings to generate quality IP human resources, including judges. Further reformation in administrative procedures in judicial system is necessary to promote judicial actions in against infringement.

4.1 Introduction

On the 14th April 2011, in the conference "Public awareness raising on IP enforcement", which was organized in Hanoi, key authorities of Vietnam, coming from Ministry of Industry and Trade, Ministry of Science and Technology, Directorate of Anti-Counterfeited goods, Custom Office, National Office of Intellectual Property met with representatives of companies, institutions, universities and intellectual property law firms to raise the public awareness on IP enforcement. In this conference, those key authorities and representatives of companies pointed out that Vietnamese IP enforcement system had yet integrated and the enforcement system was not strong enough to deter infringements. These key authorities also admitted that the enforcement teams were lack of IPR knowledge.

This chapter is constructed with 5 main sections. The first section provides evidences of IPRs enforcement in Vietnam prior to and after the accession to the WTO. The second section analyzes the strength and weakness of Vietnamese IPRs enforcement system by comparing the Vietnamese IPRs enforcement system with the system of US and France. The third section presents the strategies what Vietnamese authorities have recently been done to improve the IPRs enforcement. The fourth section analyzes 40 IP infringement cases, which involved with different types of IP. The analysis focuses on the types of actions, which IP owners would proceed to stop infringement, and the average time duration that is normally needed to solve each type of infringement. Furthermore, the outcomes of those infringed cases are discussed in respect to the amount of fine, recidivism of infringement and deterrence of similar actions. In this section, one comprehensive infringement case is described and analyzed to illustrate the strengths and weaknesses of the judicial system and enforcement system in Vietnam. This case further confirmed the discussions in the above sections. The final part of this paper provides concluding remarks with implications to policy makers to reform both judicial system and the enforcement system to stimulate and encourage innovation.

4.2 Intellectual Property Rights (IPRs) in Vietnam: evidences and a comparison of its enforcement system to US, France and Japan.

Change in economic regime has positively impacted economic growth of Vietnam, and pushed Vietnam toward the process of global economic integration. An important achievement was the accession of Vietnam to the WTO in the beginning of 2007. In satisfying the TRIPS's requirement, Vietnamese government had upgraded its civil law, and issued numbers of ordinances to make IPRs of Vietnam inline with the international IPRs' standards. Although, there have been improvements on IPRs enforcement system, the system is still perceived as weak and ineffective. A comparison to the enforcement systems of US and France is essential to Vietnam's authorities in considering to building up a more effective working enforcement system.

4.2.1 IPRs enforcement in Vietnam in the period prior to the accession to the WTO

Prior to the accession to the WTO, Vietnamese IPRs system had strongly been affected with the ideology of the central planned economic regime. This period witnessed the transition of Vietnam's economy from Central Planned Economy to Market Economy. This transition pushed Vietnamese authorities to make improvements to the IPRs legal system, and practices.

4.2.1.1 IPRs and their infringement prior to the civil law (1995)

Under the central planned economy system, the term property was not understood as a personal asset. So, most often the government entitled to be the IP holder, and people, who created those products, were given recognitions, such as reward certification and a remuneration based on the added profit but not exceeding the regulated amounts.

In this period, the term industrial property rights included patent, utility solution, industrial design, trademarks. Patent and utility solution were respectively regulated for 15 years and 6 years maximum of protection. Since most of the time, the state owned the IP, the transfer of their ownership; licensing; and registration for protection inside and outside of Vietnam was very limited and strictly controlled by the government. These philosophies were well reflected in the ordinance No. 31, which regulated the rules for Technical Innovation and Inventions; ordinance No.200, which regulated the rules for Utility Solution; ordinance No.201, which regulated the rules for Licensing. Under the effects of the ordinance No.31, an invention was first defined similar to today utility solution. However, its validity of protection was limited to an organization, where the inventor applied. The ordinance allowed a conversion of an Exclusive Right Patent to an Inventor Certification but not vice versa. Moreover, under these ordinance, most of the time, government was the owner of a patent or a utility solution, so the inventor could only be recognized or entitled for a monetary reward. The inventor of a utility solution could have received rewards but not exceeding 10,000VND (1.1 USD[13]), and 50,000 VND (5.5 USD) maximum for an inventor, who invented a patent. In the validity of these ordinances, NOIP reported that only one out of 460 patent applications filed was granted as Exclusive Right Patent (Phan, 2009). Based on those definitions and regulated definition in this period, the term infringement was almost not exist. Therefore, enforcement of an infringed act was limited to administrative punishment (warning and degrading the salary's rank). Infringed act could also be criminally prosecuted but it was related to smugglings, or extreme low quality of counterfeited goods.

The "Doi moi" changed the economic regime, and in the transitional processes, the concept of private property had been gradually emerged. The initial outcomes were reflected in the issuances of the numbers of ordinances that extended the subjectivities of protection and gradually raised the private ownership of intellectual property. Later on, in 1995 the intellectual property rights were regulated in the civil code of Vietnam. This decision explicitly recognized the intellectual property rights as civil rights that enabled authorities to create legal bindings for infringement's enforcement system.

4.2.1.2 IPRs and their infringement after the issuance of civil law in 1995

As IPRs were recognized as civil rights, and Vietnam submitted its application to become a member of the WTO, more improvements on the IPRs had been done. The ordinance No.63, which was issued in 1996, brought the IPRs of Vietnam closer to international standards. The maximum lengths of protection were extended to 20 years for a patent and 10 years for a utility solution. The emerging of open market system led the way for inventors to file for Exclusive Right Patent. As the result, more and more intellectual property applications were granted to individuals for protections. In 1997 alone, NOIP received 156 complaints for IPRs' infringement, and this number rose to 239 complaints in 1998. Under this pressure, in 1999 the government issued the ordinance No.12, which regulated the rules in handling infringement administratively. This ordinance was very important, which defined the power of different levels of authorities and procedures in handling infringements (see Appendix 1). However, its enforcement was considered not strong enough to deter infringements. For example, in this ordinance, if the infringed value of an

---

[13] Exchange rate in 1981: 1USD was approximately equal to 9,050VND (information was collected from State Bank of Vietnam).

infringement was less than 1 million VND (about 84USD14) then the parties negotiated with each other, if it could not be negotiate, then the authority in that location decided the compensation. For infringement's value was more than 1 million VND (84 USD) and if the parties could not reach an agreement for compensation, then they could bring the case to the civil court. The problem with this ordinance when it clearly stated that in the case if one party was committed to an act of infringement, the party would have to pay for a fine at the latest one year from the infringed date, or two years for infringement relating to production or manufacturing. Moreover, in the event if the infringed party did not pay the fine, then the infringed party might have to obligate to destroy the infringed products or goods that might cause harmful to human health (ordinance 12, 1999). Additionally, this ordinance also set the highest value that an authorised officer could fine, to 100 millions VND (about 8,400 USD) and the regulated authority could withdraw business license temporarily or permanently depending on how serious the infringement could impact. Over all, these administrative regulations created difficulties for authorised officers to enforce the infringement strictly and effectively.

Although, criminal prosecutions related to author rights and industrial property rights were granted in criminal code of Vietnam. The government took strong actions against producing or manufacturing counterfeited goods. As the matter of fact, most criminal measures were prosecuted against the counterfeited acts (see Table 4.1).

Table 4.1 A summary of criminal prosecution for infringements in the period of 1995-2000

Infringed activity	1995	1996	1997	1998	1999	Total
Violated Author rights, patent infringement	0	0	0	0	0	**0**
Produced, traded counterfeited goods	55	68	62	124	78	**387**
Mislead customer	0	0	0	1	1	**2**
Violated acts in publishing	1	0	0	1	2	**4**

Source: Nguyen V. Luat, Reality of handling violations in intellectual property rights in Vietnam, Intellectual property right conference organized by JICA, Hanoi 2001.

---

[14] 1USD~ 11,900 VND (Source: State Bank of Vietnam)

More serious measures were taken by the government, the criminal law issued in 1999 explicitly granted prosecution for violation in:

- Author rights and copyrights
    - o infringement of author right (article 131, criminal law).
    - o in violation of rules in publishing books, journal, medias, and others (article 271, criminal law).
- Industrial property rights
    - o producing, manufacturing, and trading counterfeited goods (article 156, criminal law).
    - o producing, manufacturing, and trading counterfeited goods, which are foods and medicines (article 157, criminal law).
    - o producing, manufacturing, and trading counterfeited goods, which are pesticide, fertilizers, and animal feeding products (article 158, criminal law).
    - o infringing the industrial property rights (article 171, criminal law).
    - o misleading customer (article 170, criminal law)

Using TRIPS's requirements as criteria for developing IPRs in Vietnam, the government continued to improve the existing IPRs and also produce more ordinances to make IPRs of Vietnam conforming to TRIPS's requirements. The ordinance No. 54, which was issued in 2000, regulated further subjectivities of protection; the subject matters of protection were extended to Trade secret, Geographical indication, Trade name, and Unfair competition. By 2005, the national assembly of Vietnam agreed to build a separated intellectual property law, which was based on the incorporation and improvement of the IP section in the civil law with other issued ordinances. Finally, the intellectual property law, which was launched in 2005 and enacted on the 1st July 2006, was considered almost identical to the TRIPS. The only two rights, which were not covered for protection, were rental rights and textile designs (Yoon and Tran, 2011). Under this law, an infringement could be solved by one of the following legal methods: administration; civil action (negotiation, civil court); prosecution (criminal court). Moreover, this law also allowed certain authorities to have the power to issue interim injunction or preliminary injunction in certain conditions.

Under administrative procedures, a number of authorised agencies have been allowed to carry out administrative measure against infringements. Those authorised agencies are: Inspectorate Department of Science and Technology (Ministry of Science and Technology); Market Control Department (Ministry of Industry and Commerce); Custom Office (Ministry of Finance); Inspectorate Department of Ministry of Culture, Tourism and Sports; Ministry of National Security; People Committees. The power of each officer in these agencies was first defined in the ordinance No.12 (see Appendix 4 for details). Despite the government's effort in fighting infringements, infringements' activities have continually grown, and they seemed to become common. Table 4.2 below presents statistical data for a number of infringements cases received by NOIP for the period of 1997 to 2010. However, these figures only reflected a very small portion of the total infringements in Vietnam. According to the head inspector of Department of Science and Technology, Ministry of Science and Technology-Vietnam, in 2006, the market control management had solely handled 12,885 cases related to selling counterfeited goods, and issued a total fine equivalent to 4.387 billions Dong (276,034 USD). This means that on average, a given fine was valued to about 21 USD. This amount of fine might be a lot in comparison to a public servant's salary, but its value was possibly very much less than the value of infringed goods. Although, administrative actions have been exercised mainly by authorized agents, they were considered not strong enough to deter infringed acts.

Table 4.2 Appeals against infringements of Industrial Property received by NOIP

Year	1997	1998	1999	2000	2001	2002	2003	2004	2005	2006	2007	2008	2009	2010
Patent& Utility Patent				1	2	9	23	33	41	17	7	5	7	4
Industrial Design	32	20	41	60	93	108	53	65	210	264	92	244	99	90
Trade marks	124	219	110	119	198	282	278	306	324	320	67	84	82	89
Total	**156**	**239**	**151**	**180**	**293**	**399**	**354**	**404**	**575**	**601**	**166**	**333**	**188**	**183**

Source: NOIP(2011)

Even though, NOIP is not authorized to provide administrative punishment to the act of infringement, it is obligated to provide examination in infringement cases. As table 4.2 shows that, the number of appeals against infringement had risen in the period of 1997 to 2006. This might indicate that people's awareness on the ownership rights has increased and they start fighting for their legal benefits. As infringement became more frequent and more sophisticated, in 2006, NOIP was divided into two organizations (NOIP and Vietnam Intellectual Property Research Institute (VIPRI). NOIP is still responsible for industrial property registrations and whereas, VIPRI is responsible for examination of granted industrial property in case of conflict of interests.

4.2.2 IPRs enforcement in Vietnam after the accession to the WTO

In adherence to the commitment of the government to TRIPS' requirements, authorities of Vietnam further improve the intellectual property law and its enforcement. As the result, the intellectual property law was amended in 2009, and its enforcement has been strengthened.

In comparison to the IP law in 2005, the amended version of 2009 improved the following main points:

- Author rights and relating to author rights
  - o increase the length of protection from 50 years to 75 years for movie, photograph, and applied arts calculating from the first publication.
  - o increase the length of protection from 50 years to 100 years for movie, photograph, and applied arts, if those have not been placed in public within 25 years since their formation.
  - o broadcasting agencies must pay royalty for the owner of author right.
- Industrial property rights
  - o extend the length for substantive examination for:
  - o a patent from 12 months to 18 months,
  - o a trademark from 6 months to 9 months, and
  - o an industrial design from 6 months to 7 months.
- Filing date is the priority date (prior to this ordinance, publication date is often used as the priority date.)
- Administrative enforcement
  - o infringed   parties   can   be   fined   administratively   without

acknowledgement or notification of infringement from IP's owners.

- o the highest amount can be up to 500 millions Dong (about 24,000 USD[15])

Despite the effort of the government, IPRs' infringements are remaining high. Enforcement system is still considered as weak and ineffective. The maximum amount of a fine for an infringement which was regulated to 500 million Dong, has been criticized a lot from firms, enterprises, and others. Their arguments were related to the value of infringed goods. As, the matter of fact, many infringed goods, which have high value, have been massively produced. So, for these cases, the amount of 500 millions Dong is not strong enough to stop infringement. The previous rule was considered better, since it allowed the maximum amount of fine could be 5 times of the value of infringed goods. Although it was also criticized for the ambiguity in the meaning of the value of "infringed goods" or the value of "goods being infringed", it shows a sense of punitive damage. This problem was raised due to a big gap in the price of "infringed goods" and the value of "goods being infringed".

A recent estimation of a market research in 2010, on average, there were about one million fake motorbikes were selling on the Vietnamese market, and 50% of those motorbikes infringed the Honda's industrial design protections (Vu, Nguyen and Nguyen, 2010). Infringements have become hot issues recently, when local firms started realizing intellectual properties are their assets. With the current capacity of the enforcement agencies, and judicial system, Vietnam will be facing many challenges in fighting for infringements. More analysis on enforcement capacity of Vietnam will be discussed in section 4 of this paper.

4.3 IPRs enforcement system in Vietnam: A comparison to US and France.

Vietnam and France's IP laws are based on civil law, so the principle of the enforcement for IPRs' infringement is to get compensation for damages. In contrast, US's IP law is based on common law, so the principle of the enforcement for IPRs' infringement is punitive damages. This explains why the granted fine in US is often very high, whereas the granted fine in Vietnam and France is normally less than the actual loss.

The enforcement systems in Vietnam, France, and US support self negotiation,

---

[15] 1 USD~20,850 VND (http://www.vietcombank.com.vn/exchangerates/Default.aspx, exchange rate for the 19/5/2011)

and judicial enforcement. However, the government of Vietnam regulated an extra method for enforcement which is administrative method. Under the administrative approach, certain authorities are granted the rights to take administrative actions quickly. As presented above, these administrative actions have been mainly exercised in IPRs' enforcement in Vietnam.

France and the US are developed countries, where their IPRs system and IP law have been enacted for many decades. So most of the courts are competent to handle IPRs' infringements. Their laws also allow suspected infringed goods to be seized or if necessarily the court can also issue a preliminary injunction prior to the trial under certain conditions. Although the IPRs' system and IP law are still new to authorities and judicial system in Vietnam, they are almost conform to TRIPS. The IP law in Vietnam is also equipped with number of tools, which can be used prior to the trial, such as: seize of infringed goods; preliminary injunction.

Unlike some countries, Vietnam and the US do not organize a separate court system for handling IPRs infringement. However, there are 10 "tribunaux de grande instance" throughout of France, where judges are specialized to deal with the IPRs' infringement, so it is recommended to settle IPRs' infringement in one of these specialized courts. Differently, in the US, a claimant may choose any district court to start a law suit against IPRs' infringement. This freedom has also raised a question on the quality of the court (Ishihara, 2008). In contrast for Vietnam, the plaintiff must first file a law suit in the district court in the plaintiff's resident location. If the plaintiff is a foreigner, then it is allowed and recommended to file a law suit in the people court of Hanoi or Ho Chi Minh city.

There are certain tools, IP owners could use to stop infringement immediately before the trial. In the case of Vietnam, IP's owner can contact administrative authorities to seize the goods, if the goods might possibly be dispersed. This activity is almost identical with France; the only different is the bailiff takes actions to seize the goods. Furthermore, a preliminary injunction can be granted immediately, if a law suit has been filed and a deposit has been paid (see table 4.3). In France and the US, a preliminary injunction can only be issued after a hearing and the judge see that the evidences, which are shown by the claimant, satisfied a number of regulated conditions.

In collecting evidences for the trial, all three countries accept self collection of evidences, but those evidences, which are collected by authorities, are more convincible, and more enforceable in the case of France. Therefore, in the case of

France, it is legally recommended to consult with a lawyer to assign a bailiff to handle the collection of evidences.

Since, Vietnam and France's laws are based on civil law system, so for an infringement case, the court normally assesses the damages and awards a compensation in principle of recovery. In contrast, the US's law is based on common law, so punitive damage is allowed. Therefore, an infringer may have to pay much more than the damages found. The ordinance No.106 of Vietnam, which was issued in 2006 allow punitive damages, since the compensation could be as much as five times of the infringed goods' value. However, the ordinance No.97, which was issued in 2010, limited the maximum amount of compensation to VND 500 millions.

Table 4.3 A comparison of IP enforcement system of Vietnam, France and the US

Criteria	Vietnam	France	United States of America
Law system	Civil law	Civil law	Common law
	First to file	First to file	First to invent
Methods of handling infringement	• Negotiation • Administrative procedure • Civil procedure • Criminal procedure	• Negotiation • Civil procedure • Criminal procedure	• Negotiation • Civil procedure • Criminal procedure
Separated IP court	No	No	No
Judicial system	• District people court • Provincial people court • High people court	• "Tribunaux de grande instance"	• District court • Appeal court • Supreme court
Assess the experiences of Judges in handling IP's dispute	Lack of experiences	Experiences	Experiences
Tools to stop infringement's activities pre-trial.	• Seize the goods • Preliminary injunction (without hearing)	• Seize with support of the bailiff and a deposit • Preliminary	• Temporary restraining order • Preliminary injunction (after

Criteria	Vietnam	France	United States of America
	o Pay a deposit ~ 20% seized goods	injunction (after hearing)	hearing)
Burden of proof	Yes	Yes	Yes
Contributory infringement	Yes	Yes	Yes
Method for collecting evidences	• self collection of evidences. • collection of evidences with the support of public authorities	• self collection of evidences with the support of a bailiff. • collection of evidences with the support of public authorities	• self collection of evidences. • collection of evidences with the support of public authorities
Method for assessing damages	Compensation	Compensation	Punitive compensation o the award can not be less than the sum of (royalty fee + interest + costs of litigation) o treble damages.

Source: Own construction with references to Hemphill(2008), Baker and Mc Kenzie (2007)

4.4 How has Vietnam strengthened its IPRs system?

Since 1995, the IP system of Vietnam has been continually improved. The conformance of IP law with TRIPS's requirements and the raising people' awareness on the IPRs proves that Vietnam has strengthened its IPRs system. This achievement was gained by the commitment of the government, tighter coordination of responsible agencies, and contribution of knowledgeable staffs. Reaching to this state, the government has launched a strategic action plan since 2005, which targeted number of objectives, including: improvement of the IP law and its enforcement; raising awareness of IPRs in enterprises and in the communities; leveraging capacity of human resource.

4.5 Leveraging knowledge of IPRs in society

Pursuing the strategic action plan, the Prime Minister issued a Decision (68/2005/QĐ-TTg) to launch a program with its aim was to leveraging the awareness of business enterprises on the IPRs. A board management of this program was formed with the leading of Vice Minister of MOST, and other members, who are Vice Ministers of MOET, MOF, MARD, MOCI, MOH, MOJ, and MOCST. This committee was formed with key important authorities to ensure the integration of the program. This program has been well known as program CT168, whose objectives were: leveraging the awareness of business enterprises in the field of intellectual property rights; increasing the competitive capacity of Vietnamese enterprises.

In the implementation of this program, the government reserved a budget of 10 billions dong for the year 2006, and about 28 billions and 12 billions subsequently for the year 2007 and 2008 (MOST, 2009). Those budgets were provided to cover expenditures for common activities of the program and for the implementation of the granted projects (see table 4.4). After three years of implementation, the program CT168 had successfully:

- built an working scheme for the operation and integration

- promulgated the knowledge of IP and IPRs over national TV channel, radio station, workshops, conferences, and studies' tours. Those activities were attracted over 1,100 enterprises, and more than 100 colleges and universities to attend.

- leveraged the competitiveness of products with geographical indications' protections.

In spite of the achievements, program CT168's phase 1 showed its weaknesses, which should be improved. Table 4.4 provides that the budget was not well utilized as planned. Only 6% of the total budget was consumed in the first year, 29% in the second year, and 63% for the third year. In total for three years, only one third of the budget was spent for the whole program. This might indicate that the plan was not well designed, and probably the program was short of human resources in carrying out projects. The amounts of spending for program's activities were accounted from 10 to 35 percentages of the expenditures, which might indicated that the program was not well integrated and coordinated.

85

Table 4.4 Budget and expenditure for program 168

Program CT168	2006		2007		2008		Total	
	VND*	USD	VND*	USD	VND*	USD	VND*	USD
Authorised Budget	**10,000**	**625,000**	**28,226.44**	**1,764,153**	**12,345.58**	**771,599**	**50,572**	**3,160,751**
Program's activities	1,000	62,500	1,500	93,750	2,717	169,813	5,217	326,063
Implementation of projects	9,000	562,500	26,726.44	1,670,403	9,628.58	601,786	45,355	2,834,689
Consumed Expenditure	**596.57**	**37,286**	**8,177.76**	**511,110**	**7,785.85**	**486,616**	**16,560**	**1,035,011**
Program's activities	596.57	37,286	827.79	51,737	2,703.26	168,954	4,128	257,976
Implementation of projects	-		7,349.97	459,373	5,082.59	317,662	12,433	777,035
Percentages of project expense	0%		90%		65%		75%	
Expenditure over Budget (%)	6%		29%		63%		33%	

(*) Vietnamese currency is calculating in million dong.

Exchange rate: 1 USD~16,000 VND.
Source: Ministry of Science and Technology, Report on program "assisting enterprises for intellectual property development", 17/7/2009.

Program CT168's phase 1 finished in 2010, the government concluded that it achieved the targeted objectives and the government has approved the 2nd phase for the period of 2011-2015. In this phase, the program will be focusing on:

- establishment and assisting IP consulting organizations
- assisting in development of procedures in managing scientific researches and their products
- assisting in exploration of scientific, technical information, patent's information, and technology spill-over for researching, manufacturing, and trading purposes

- assisting in implementing programs and activities relating to IP enforcement, actions against infringements

Based on the achievement in the first phase and the targets of the second phase of the program CT168, the awareness of society and business society will surely be raised. The successful outcomes of this program will ultimately strengthen the IPRs' system in Vietnam.

4.6 Building capacity of human resource

Vietnam is currently facing with the shortage of qualified human sources in intellectual property. This shortage can be seen in the judicial system, and can be evaluated through training curriculums. These problems will be ceased, if it would get adequate attentions of responsible authorities.

Judicial system: According to Mr. Tien, a judge of High people court of Vietnam, that the court system is currently short of judges, who has experiences and systematic trainings on IP. As the matter of fact, that the IPRs are still new to many judges in Vietnam, and not many district courts and provincial courts are capable of handling IP disputes easily. In the near future, this system would need at least 500 capable judges, who have capacity in handling IP matter.

Training curriculum: Course on intellectual property rights still receives inadequate attentions from many universities and Ministry of Education and Training in Vietnam. Since 2006, the University of Social Science and Humanities (the National University) in Vietnam has been the only one providing a bachelor degree in intellectual property. Although, each year leading universities of laws and Judicial Academy provide few thousands legal officers, hundreds of judges and lawyers, their teaching curriculum contains only one or two courses of 2 credit teaching hours[16] on the topic of IPRs. Other universities, the topic of intellectual property might have been introduced as a small topic in a number of courses, such as: international economics; technology transfer; standardization. Under this circumstance, NOIP has coordinated with different organizations, institutions, and enterprises to provide short training or professional training on IP and IPRs (Spoo and Dao, 2010). As, the results, thousands of people, and officers have attended these training courses since 2004. Not only has this contribution leveraged the awareness of people on IP and IPRs, it has also enlarged the capacity of officers in handling IP's infringements.

Program CT168's phase 2 has put training on IP and IPRs as one of its main

---

[16] 2 credit teaching hours is equivalent to 30 teaching hours in a semester.

target. Since 2004, we also seen more universities and colleges have integrated the topic on IP and IPRs in their teaching curriculum. More scholarship programs have been reserved for qualified students to get abroad to study at graduate levels training on IP. All of these actions have been integrated to ensure that we would have adequate human resources capacity in handling IPRs infringement in the future. As these infringements are getting more systematic and sophisticated.

4.7 Case studies and Lessons learned

As presented in the above section, administrative measure is the most common action, which has been exercised against IP infringement in Vietnam. Nevertheless, a small number of infringements have been brought to civil court or even prosecuted. Although, there is no database for the infringements existing in Vietnam, this research has been able to collect 40 infringement cases of all IP types with reasonable details, which can be used for analysis. These cases show the weaknesses and incompleteness of the Vietnamese administrative and judicial system in handling IP's infringements. In the first part of this section, basic statistics about the cases are going to be summarized, and learned lessons are going to be presented. In the second part, a detail of a utility patent infringement case, which was first brought to civil court to claim for the exclusive right, is going to be summarized and analyzed. The analysis of this case enhances the discussion and argument, which have brought up in the previous sections.

4.7.1 IP infringements, how they have been settled

The above section has provided the mechanism, which has been applying in Vietnam business environment in resolving and settling the IP infringements. The data for infringement cases have been collected from three sources: MOST[17]; NOIP[18]; and NCO[19]. Although, there have been a lot infringement cases, only limited number of cases have been briefly documented by those three sources. Among these cases, we then need to cases, which have enough details for our analysis. Therefore, the completeness is the first criteria, which we have to consider in the selection process. Then, up to next step, we consider different stake holders (owner, infringer, authorities) to include in our analysis. So, after the selection process, only 40 cases have been selected, among them six patents & utility solution cases, 10 industrial design cases, 20 trademarks cases, and 4 copyright cases have

---

[17] MOST is responsible for issues relating to industrial property

[18] NOIP handles the registrations

[19] NCO is responsible for problems relating to copyrights

been chosen (see Appendix 5, 6, 7, 8). These cases reflect well different types of IP infringements, which have been existed in the businesses' practices in Vietnam. Although, these infringement cases do not provide the most representative picture of IP enforcement in Vietnam, these indicate the weakness of the enforcement system and therefore, they can be lessons to learn for many firms in handling IP infringements. The following section provides some basic statistics of the cases, and then the analysis focuses on different aspects, such as: types of settlement; time duration of a case; method for evaluation; amount of a fine; consistency between decisions; roles of different stake holders.

4.7.2 Types of settlement

In Vietnam, there are four different ways, which can be exercised to resolve an infringement: negotiation; administrative measure; civil procedure; criminal procedure. Negotiation happens when the two parties reach an agreement on a dispute without any decision generated from an administrative body or a court order. Whereas, any action or decision, which is generated from any of the administrative authorities (see appendix 4), is considered as administrative measure. Furthermore, civil procedure happens when the two parties could not reach a consensus, so they have to request for the civil court's resolution. Finally, criminal procedure is applied when the infringer is committed to a serious infringement, which have been seriously affected human health or threatened national security. In this sample, out of 40 cases, only 6 cases have been settled by civil court system, 34 cases have been solved by administrative measures and only one case is resolved through negotiation. Surprisingly, all of the foreign IP owners in this sample have chosen administrative measures to resolve their disputes. The following sections are going to provide explanations.

4.7.3 Basic statistics about the infringement cases

Table 4.5 shows that among 40 cases, there are 22 cases involving with foreign IP owners and only 2 cases involving foreign IP infringers. Most of the infringements that relate to foreign IP owners are in the area of trademarks and industrial design. These statistic data reflect the fact that foreign IP owners have increasingly filed for protections of their industrial designs and trademarks in Vietnam since the last decade. Unlike the industrial designs and trademarks, which can be infringed easily, utility patents and patents are much harder to infringe, because they require technical competencies and know how, so fewer cases have been reported in these areas. Noticeably, most of foreign IP owners are large firms and well known, whereas most of the domestic infringers are small size firms.

4.7.4 Time duration for IP infringement settlement

Although, the length, which is required to solve an IP infringement, is very much depended on the nature of the IP infringement, the complexity (including technology, political support...etc.) of the cases, it seems that the quickest way to settle a dispute is to utilize an administrative procedure. As table 4.5 shows that on average the time needed to settle a dispute through an administrative procedure is between 1 to 6 months or even less. At a different approach, IP infringements can also be brought to court for settlement or prosecuted. Table 4.5 provides that for the same type of IP infringement, the time duration needed to solve a case through a judicial system can be over 10 times more than the time needed for administrative measure. Among the IP infringement types, Patent and Utility solution infringement take the longest time to resolve the issue. This can be explained by the nature of the Patent or Utility solution, which is often more complexity than other types of infringement. Resolving a trademark infringement possibly takes a long time, as it is shown in the table 4.5, the average time duration needed is just shorter than the time duration needed for the case of patent and utility solution. Industrial design seemingly requires least time for the settlement.

Table 4.5 Summary Cases on IP infringement.

Type of Infringement	Patent & Utility Solution	Industrial Design	Trademark	Copyright
Total Infringement	6	10	20	4
Foreign IP Owner	1	5	13	3
Foreign IP Infringer	0	1	0	0
Average of administrative settlement's duration (days)	146	33	47	45
Average of court settlement's duration (days)	1,882	314	685	
Types of settlements				
Administration	3	8	18	4
Civil court	2	2	2	0
Criminal court	0	0	0	0
Negotiation	1	0	0	0
Fines				
Average amount of administrative fines ($USD)	1,218	2,300	2,160	4,188
Average amount of judicial fines ($USD)	17,745			

Source: Own calculation based on the Appendix 5; Appendix 6; Appendix 7; Appendix 8;

4.7.5 Method for evaluation of infringement

Evaluation the value of an infringement is not easy, since there is no explicit guideline to define a standard method for assessment. In addition to that, the definition on the law about the value of an infringement is also ambiguous. As the law has stated "value of the infringed goods", authorities have interpreted the meaning differently and applied inconsistent actions. So there have been arguments on "is it the value of a real product?" or "is it the value of a fake one?" As in the case of Louis Vuitton, since the value of the fake goods is very much smaller than the value of the real one (see appendix 7). Obviously, in this case the values of the infringed goods were interpreted as the value of the fake goods. The argument is very much relevantly impacted on the power of the enforcement. Moreover, different interpretations and standardized method for evaluation make unfair judgments. Even more dangerous, it would create a loop hole in the enforcement system.

4.7.6 Amount of a fine

Out of 40 cases presented: 21 cases were given fines, which were less than or equal to 30 millions VND (1,622 USD[20]); 3 cases were given fines, which were more than 100 millions VND (5,400 USD); 8 cases were given fines, which were between 30 millions VND to 100 millions VND; 8 cases were given only injunctive relieves (see Appendix 5, 6, 7, 8). This statistical data shows that the amount of fines is very small comparing to the loss or potential damages. However, this reflects the spirit of the ordinances, which are presented in the Appendix 4. The worst case, which can be happened in the administrative measures or even in civil court, is the loss of business license and a fine of a maximum value of 500 millions VND (27,027 USD). Even, in this scenario, the fine is meaningless to many infringers. Because, in the case a business's license is withdrawn, the business can likely get another business license for the cost of a couple of hundred dollars. Moreover, such small value of the maximum fine, which is authorized by law, does not motivate IP owners to bring their case for trials.

Based on the above arguments, the law should reflect that the amount of the fine should at least cover the damages caused by the infringement. Heavier fines can also be applied. However, the idea behind the law is not to make infringers out of their businesses unless infringers repeatedly recidivate their infringements. The amount of fine can be determined in accordance with the argument proposed by

---

[20] Exchange rate for 2010: 1USD=18,500 VND approximately.

Benzoni (2001). As it should cover the loss of profits and plus an extra amount of penalty, which is limited to the loss due to loss of monopolistic price and loss in quantity of good sold. Therefore, the amount of fine is limited to about two and half of the value of the real goods. This amount is large enough to cover the damage and probably does not often make the infringer out of business. To prevent the recidivism of the act of infringement, heavier fine should be considered for the repeated cases.

4.7.7 Reactions of IP owners

There are 15 different foreign IP's owners in the sample. Most of these IP foreign owners are well known not only in Vietnam, but also in the world, such as Honda, Coca cola, Cisco, Denone, Louis Vuitton...etc. A few infringement cases have also associated with international disputes, such as the case of Duy Loi Hammock. Furthermore, disputes between domestics IP owners and domestic IP infringers are also brought to this discussion.

As explained in the previous section, IP owners hesitate to bring the cases to court due to the complexity, bureaucratic paper work, and small value of the compensation. Evidently, in our sample, there are about more than a dozen infringement cases relating to foreign IP owners, none of these cases has been brought for trial. This reaction is also true for domestic IP owners. This again confirms that administrative measure has been favorably exercised over the court settlement.

IP owners may face dilemmas in choosing the right strategy to handle infringements due to factors, which have been discussed above. These dilemmas reflect well through the case of Tien Thinh (see appendix 5) and Honda (see appendix 6). As in these cases, the infringements are not reduced after the administrative settlements, but they are seemingly expanded wider. This problem was well described as "living together with flooding".

4.8 Illustrated civil court case-The Brick making machine case.

4.8.1 Introduction to inventor and his utility patent

Mr. Hoang Thinh, an owner of a small private mechanic production site companies at the Krongana District of Daklak province. At the end of 1990s and beginning of the year 2000, many brick manufacturing sites often used a brick making machine in producing bricks in replacement for traditional manual labor production. Although, this machine does not look attractive, it had functions of mixing and pressing to make brick firm and smooth. Moreover, this kind of machine could produce about 1,200 bricks per hour with 7 workers, which is far more than number of bricks these workers could have produced manually. So, this kind of machine has been widely used in many places through out Vietnam.

However, there have been a number of concerns in using this machine. First of all, it was considered as unsafe machine. In the process of mixing clay, this machine requires workers to use their hands or foot to push the clay into the mixing area. This activity is considered as risky, if workers were reluctant to this job just for a second, or if they become tired after hours of working, they might put their foot or hands in this mixer. Consequently, it is hard for one could image, workers might lost their foot or hands. The second issue, this kind of machine could not utilize stones mixed in the clay, so when there is a stone in the clay, the mixing process is disrupted as the stone is needed to be taken out; it leads to time and oil consuming.

After 10 years of studying different kinds of brick making machines, and utilizing his knowledge about machinery, which he earned from his bachelor degree in mechanical engineering, he has produced a brick making machine. This machine has an axial rake, which could automatic take the clay from a tray then put the clay into the mixing area. Furthermore, this machine can also crush stones, so the machine can work continually without disruption. Not only did this device make the machine safer to use, it increased the capacity of the machine and quality of the produced brick. It also saved oils consumption and reduced number of labors needed. Table 4.6 presents the advantage of the new machine over the old one.

Table 4.6 Advantage of the new invented brick making machine over the old one

Criteria	Before	After
Number of workers needed	7	5
Accident prevention	No	Yes
Better quality of bricks produced	No	Yes
Output (number of bricks per hour)	1200	2500
Machine performance		25% increasing
Saving on oil consumption		1000 liters/year

Source: Information is collected from IDST of Daklak's province.

4.8.2 Fighting for the rights

Prior to 2003, not many people in big cities of Vietnam could have the knowledge about intellectual property. However, Mr. Hoang Thinh was well awarded of that, he had filed his invention at the NOIP on the 20th of August 2001 for a utility patent. About a year later, his utility patent was granted on the 20th December 2002 with 10 years of protection calculating from his filing date. So, if he pays for protection as the regulated requirement, this protection would be expired on the 19th August 2011.

At the end of the year 2002, he started producing this machine for commercial purposes. However, soon after his machines were selling in the market, he noticed that a small private mechanic production place produced a machine with similar parts and functions to his protected machine. Then later on the infringements were gone wide. There were several private mechanic production sites, which have started imitating his products and selling to market. The infringement was not just happened in his district; it has replicated to the provincial level and expanded to other neighboring provinces: Binh Duong, Binh Thuan, Binh Dinh, and Dong Nai. The following table 4.7 presents chronicle events of Mr. Thinh's activities in against infringement.

Table 4.7 Chronicle events – Brick making machine case.

Date	IP Owner	Authority's action
19/1/2003	• sent a warning to an infringer	
27/3/2003	• sent a claim to IDST of Daklak province.	
5/2003	• Broadcasting his invention in radio station three times.	
6/ 2003	• sent warnings to different infringers in the provinces of Binh Duong, Binh Thuan, Binh Dinh, and Dong Nai. • published an article about infringement of his utility patent in the Legal newspaper; and newspaper of Daklak province	
8/2003		• The head of the Krongana district sent notices to mechanical production sites, and brick production plants in the district about this

Date	IP Owner	Authority's action
		invention and the protected utility patent.
5/2004	• sent requests to NOIP for evaluation on infringements of a number of mechanic producers in Daklak	
9/2004		• NOIP sent an evaluation report to Mr. Hoang Thinh to confirm the infringement.
August to November 2004	• sent 2nd warnings to the infringers	
6/10/2004	• sent a claim to DIST of Daklak province	
21/12/2004		• Deputy director of IDST Daklak requested the head of Krongana's district to take actions to 14 infringers.
8/2005		• Daklak's TV station broadcasting the infringement of the utility patent
10/2005		• People committee of Krongana district sent notifications to infringers and demanded to stop violation of the right.
5/2006	• sent requests to NOIP for evaluation on infringements of a number of mechanic producers in Binh Duong, Khanh Hoa, and Daklak. • sent requests to People committee of Krongana district and economic police of Daklak's province to take actions against 92 infringers in the two districts: Krongana, and KrongPak.	
7/2006		• NOIP sent an evaluation report to Mr. Hoang Thinh to confirm the infringement.
13/9/2006		• IDST of MOST sent a request to IDSTs of provinces and demand to take actions to settle the matter
20-30/11/2006		• Authorities of EaBong Ward (a ward of Krongana) and Havip IP law firm together inspected infringes in this location.
3/2/2007	• sent a request for compensation of damages to Viet My.	
8/3/2007	• sent a report to Krongana	

Date	IP Owner	Authority's action
	district and IDST of Daklak.	
31/7/2007		• IDST of Daklak formed an inspection team to investigate.
28/11/2007		• The inspection team investigated three infringers: Tan Tien Hung; Quyet Thang; VietMy. • The team confirmed the infringement.
11/2007		• IDST of Daklak sent a request to IDST of MOST to clarify the infringement and demanded the method of settlement.
28/12/2007		• IDST of MOST sent a reply.
31/12/2007		• IDST of Daklak, People committee of Krongana, and medias inspected three sites: Tan Tien Hung; Quyet Thang; Viet My.
7/1/2008		• TV broadcasting the infringement
15/1/2008		• IDST of Daklak, Hoang Thinh, Tan Tien Hung, Quyet Thang met for licensing. However, it was not successful.
20/2/2008		• IDST of Daklak sent a request to People committee of Daklak province to solve the matter
24/3/2008		• People committee of Daklak province demanded the People court of Daklak to solve the matter.
24/6/2008	• file a law suit	
20/8/2008		• request all party to be at the court on the 26/8/2008 for trial.
26/8/2008-4/2010		• Postponed the trial for more than 15 times for different reasons. • 11/11/2008 the provincial people court issued a decision to postpone the case to seek for consultancy from High people court.
17/6/2010		• The court awarded the winning of the case to Mr. Hoang Thinh. • Request infringer to pay: 351 millions VND for infringement' compensation to Mr. Hoang Thinh; 61 millions VND for lawyers.

4.8.3 Why is the invention attractive to infringers?

The brick making machine of Mr. Hoang Thinh not only has advantages in safety operation, but it also generates better economic benefit to infringers. The following data provides the advantages of the patented brick making machine over the regular machines (see table 4.8).

On average a brick producer earns 150VND for each brick sold. Let us assume that a brick producer would minimum operate with the following data:

- Working weeks per year: 40 weeks

- Working days: 5 days/ week

- Working hours: 5 hours/ day

- Worker's salary: 2 millions VND/month for 12 months in a year.

- USD/VND exchange rate: 19,500

- Oil price: VND 10,000/ liter

Bricks produced yearly= number of bricks produced per hour * No. working hours/ day * No. working days/ week * No. working weeks/year.

Table 4.8 A comparison of production capacities of the two machines

Category	Without invention	With invention
Bricks produced yearly (brick)	1,200,000	2,500,000
Worker (person)	7	5
Oil saving (liter)	None	1000

Base on the above data and assumption, the economic benefit could then be calculated as showing in the following table 4.9:

Table 4.9 Economic benefit generating with the application of new invention.

Category	Without invention		With invention	
	Million VND	USD	Million VND	USD
Profit from selling produced bricks	252	12,923	525	26,923
Oil saving			10	513
Workers' salary	168	8,615	120	6,154
Profit before tax	**84**	4,308	**415**	21,282
Profit after tax (Corporate tax 25%)	63	3,231	**311.25**	**15,962**
Difference on profit			248.25	12,731

With the application of the new invention, the brick producer could earn extra 12,731 USD/year in minimum. Therefore, profit generated for 7 years of infringement could be as much as 89,117 USD. This well explains why the invention was so attractive to infringers.

4.8.4 Comments on Administrative and Judicial approaches in this case

This case was lasting for more than 7 years with the participations of many different levels of authorities, from local authorities to national authorities, and with involvement of different public media. This case was considered as the longest IP case dispute in Vietnam. Frankly speaking, one might not understand why a utility patent with 10 years of protection (actually 9 years of protection) has been fought by the owner for 7 years and half to get its rights.

<u>The weakness of the administrative system</u>

Since IP infringement can be solved by administrative procedure, so Mr. Thinh has made requests to the IDST of Daklak, IDST of MOST, and people committee at various levels to fight for infringements. Legally, any of these administrative authorities could have given fines to those infringers. Even through the effect might not be wide, it could create barrier for new infringers. If the case was solved by administrative procedure at the highest level of authorities: Head of province or Chief inspector of IDST (MOST) in the years:

- between 2004-2006, Mr. Thinh could have received VND100 millions maximum for the compensation of damages; or

- between of the year 2007-2009, he could have received the compensation as much as 5 times of the value of infringed goods; or

- for the year 2010 he could get a maximum of VND 500 millions.

However, in this case, no single administrative fine was issued and it took more than 5 years for the case to be passed to the court. This illustrates that administrative procedure sometimes can be lengthy and complex matter.

Comments on the judicial procedure

The case was handled to the court on the 24th June 2008, and Mr. Thinh received a request order to be in the court for the trial on the 26th August 2008. However, it was later cancelled and he received not less than 12 other request orders from court to set for the trial in different times; however they were all cancelled due to many reasons. For almost of the request orders, Mr. Thinh had to travel 30km from his house to the people court and his lawyer had to fly 6 times from HoChiMinh city to his province just to receive a notification of cancellation. Finally, the trial was organized on the 17th June 2010, almost two years from the first request order. In this court, he won the case and an amount of VND 351 millions was ordered to compensate for the infringement and another amount of VND 61 millions was ordered to compensate Mr.Thinh's lawyer fees. Although, this amount set the highest record for IP infringement compensation in Vietnam at the present, Mr. Thinh and his lawyer should deserve to get more.

After 7 years and half, the case was finally settled with a great effort of Mr. Thinh. Frankly speaking, when hearing this story, no one would imagine that they would be patient enough to follow these unbelievable administrative and judicial processes. This case explains why IP infringements have been popular in Vietnam, and not many cases have been brought to courts each year.

4.9 Concluding remarks and implications to IPRs policy maker

Vietnam has been facing with an increasing number of infringements, although it has regularly improved its IP and its enforcement law. There are two most important reasons, which can explain. First of all, the knowledge on IPR has not been widely promulgated and the practice of imitation has been vastly accepted among people and firms. Secondly, it is about the law itself, which needs to be further reformed. Facing with that Vietnam has implemented a number of strategic reinforcing actions, including: issuances of ordinances to provide regulations and guidelines in handling IPRs infringement administratively; raising the IP awareness of the society; strengthening IPRs human resource capacity.

Since the year 1995, the government of Vietnam has continually introduced IP laws and their amendments. The ordinance No. 63, the ordinance No. 106, and recently the ordinance No.97 have not only regulated in details the power of the assigned authority in fighting for infringements, they have also enlarged their scopes of protection. Although, the responsibilities and powers of each level of authorities have been defined, the conflicts of roles and power of authorities in different legal documents have still existed. Additionally, lack of integration between authorities has created pathways for infringers to continue doing business with their infringed acts.

In promoting IP awareness to the society, a number of programs have been launched since 2005. Although their organizing scheme was not good, but a number of their main activities have been well implemented. Especially, the promulgated activities have been evaluated as impressive. Training activities on IP has been still limited. IP and IPRs knowledge is still not yet implemented in the university, even at the leading universities.

The summary of selected cases confirmed that administrative procedures have been the most preferable method in handling IP disputes in Vietnam. It generally takes shorter time and provides immediate effects. However, it showed that authorities rarely exercise full their powers in handling these cases. Cases were handled by the judicial system takes much longer time. The illustrated case on the brick making machine provided a good example of the complexity of administrative system and judicial system in handling IPRs infringement.

Based on the above findings, in short term, the government of Vietnam should continue to reinforce and strengthen the administrative procedures, and provide public with IPRs knowledge. Furthermore, standardized processes and interpretation should be applied in handling infringement cases. To do so, the law should provide clearer and consistent definitions for terms and methods, which used in assessing the infringement. Furthermore, the amount of fine should be limited to two and half amount of the value of the real goods, unless the infringement is recidivated or it is considered as criminal offend. Additionally, further reformation of the administrative procedure in judicial system should be implemented to allow people to get access to the judicial system easily.

In a longer term, the government should concentrate on building IP human resources. IP training activities should be widely and compulsorily provided for staff working in judicial system, custom offices, NOIP, VIPRI, economics police departments, market control management departments, and departments of science and technology. In order to do so, building up curriculums and providing systematic training at undergraduate, graduate levels, on the job training are critical. The government should consider asking foreign experts for advices and facilitation. Nevertheless, supporting programs, which are similar to program CT168, should be vitally offered to people and firms to leverage their understanding of the basic IP knowledge and enforcement. Additionally, a strategic plan should be built to transfer the administrative measure to judicial measure to bring fairness to IP owners.

CHAPTER 5. CONCLUSION AND REMARKS

The main concern through out this dissertation is how to promote innovation in given the economic condition, institutional transformation, and reformation of education, science and technology of Vietnam. The analysis has focused strictly to the predefined research objectives, which cover the manufacturing firms' characteristics and factors that support their firms' innovation, the effects of patenting cost on patenting behaviors and the effects of IPR enforcement.

Corresponding to the economic condition, industry, notably the manufacturing business sector has contributed a large portion of economic value. Therefore, this dissertation mainly focuses on manufacturing firms. Utilizing the knowledge and empirical studies of economists in the field, the analysis has relied on two data sets, one was collected by the World Bank and the other was constructed with references to the Oslo's manual and the work of Peteers and van Pottelsberghe (2003) and aim at active technological firms. The first data set, which was obtained from the World Bank, has provided a rich set of data comprising of 520 manufacturing firms with enough details for the analysis. Although this data set mainly provide firms' characteristics and some references to firm ability in turning new ideas into real products, it helps reasoning the answers to some predefined objectives. One the other hand, the second set of data was targeted at active technological, although it has only 64 firms in the total for the analysis. The emerging of the two analytical outcomes provides that innovation in manufacturing firms is positively influenced by firms' characteristics, such as: age; size; and legal business type. Further empirical analysis on firms' innovation culture suggests that rewarding scheme, supporting employees in education and training and actively participating in intellectual property related activities are the indicators for innovation. Moreover, empirical findings also confirmed that supplier, customer, university personnel and patent document are critical external resources for new ideas in active technological firms. Hence, board of management should create such policies, which not only encourage building up but also enhance firms' relationship with these external resources of ideas. Additionally, in examining of the firms ability in implementing new ideas, empirical findings implies that the average education level and supportive training programs are the determinants, which indicate firms' personnel competence in turning new ideas into new processes or products. Despite the weaknesses of the Vietnamese educational system, these empirical findings also suggest that the educational system needs to be reformed to satisfy firms' requirements.

As theoretical framework claims that patents reflect firms' innovation. However, there might be many possible reasons for innovative firms not to patent, including the cost for patenting and their belief in the principle of intellectual property right (the exclusive right). For that reasons, chapter 3 of this dissertation found that there was a traditional demand curve between cost for patenting and the volume of patent filings. This explicitly implies that the cheaper patenting cost would drive more patent filing. However, cheaper patenting cost might also lead to lower quality of patents, due to overloading work of patent examiners and other IP administrative staff in against the poor infrastructure and working condition. So, policy makers should consider the optimum solution to balance out the patenting cost and the quality of patent

In addition to the patenting cost, the enforcement of the exclusive rights might also result in the increase of patent filings for protection. Chapter 4 provided a comparison between the enforcement system of Vietnam, France and the US. The analysis of this system points out that Vietnam's enforcement system has been applied administrative measure over the judicial measure in tackling IP infringements very often. This type of measurement is quick and immediate, although it might be prone to misconduct of actions and unfairness judgments. The real infringement cases illustrate the weaknesses including time requirement in handling the matters, the small amount of fines and compensation of the both systems (administrative measure and judicial measure). This chapter outlines that both of the administrative measure and judicial measure need to be reformed and strengthened.

In response to those weaknesses, highest levels of authorities should show their commitments. Improving the working condition and infrastructure, promoting the linkage between firms and academic institutions, speeding up and spreading out the program CT168 phase II, and tightening the IP enforcement should get urgent attentions and should be done in a short term. Nevertheless, in longer term, reforming the education system, the judicial system is a must for Vietnam and it needs serious attentions and implementations. For long term success and changing in the social behaviors toward infringements, it requires the endurable patience, the firmness and strong support from key authorities in the government.

Short term solution

There are some actions can be brought right away to create immediate effects or influence the firms or individual behaviors. Since firms in Vietnam have a limited understanding on the knowledge of IP and IPRs, such program as CT168 can be very beneficial to firms and individuals. Therefore, the MOST and the NOIP should closely collaborate with department of science and technology at major economic cities and provinces to propagate the basic IP and IPRs knowledge to firms in their locations. Prior to such kind of action, a firms' survey may be vital and realistic to identify the needs of the firms in the location. Moreover, this type of actions should be organized in a sustainable way, in which an active unit in each of these locations can play a role of a consulting centre with supporting staff to answer and provide supports to firms' questions or demands on IP or IPR relating issues. Moreover, MOST and NOIP should improve its online IP database and allow freely accessible to firms and academic researchers. This helps boosting up firms' innovative ideas.

In corresponding to the issue of the linkage between universities and firms, this linkage can be established and enhanced by providing a mechanism in supporting firms in developing new products or services. This mechanism is relied on the annual funding sources, which are reserved for science and technology development. Normally, these kinds of funding resources are provided to academic researchers only. So, in order to promote the linkage between the academic researchers and industries, these funding resources should make available to both academic researchers and firms. However, the research fund only gets approval when academic researchers and firms jointly develop a new product or new process. Some percentages of the generated profits of certain years after diffusing the products or services should be contributed back to the research funds and a small portion of this profit shall be allocated to researchers.

Long term solution

Given the commitment of the authorities, a long term solution would focus on the roots of the problems, including institution, education and science technology, which have been long criticized over the past decade. First of all, the institutional framework needs to be reformed in the direction of judicial measure orientation. This means that the new systems will need consistent procedure, more quality human capital and better infrastructure. Administrative measure should only limit to identifying problems, collecting evidences, and filing for court procedure if it is necessary. In all cases, except for criminal prosecution, defendants always can pursue their cases in court for fair trials. However, this administrative action of judicial procedure must be reformed to make it easily accessible to all people. This reformation requires more competent administrative staff, judges and better supportive infrastructures. Furthermore, to make the law more enforceable higher fine and professional due care are required. Therefore, the maximum amount of fine should be changed and it is important to have a new updated teaching curriculum, which should not be apart from the reality. A systematic plan in training and retraining would generate a pool of quality human resources for the system. Furthermore, different incentive packages and punishments should be designed to maintain the professional due care of these public servants. In addition to that, different IP knowledge and judicial procedure should be promulgated widely to people through public media to increase their awareness on infringement and methods to resolve their issues.

Secondly, education, science and technology have been long concerned to policy makers. In order to satisfy the need of the society and sustainable development, education system should be dynamic and quality. The term dynamic reflects that the education system should be designed to support the development of businesses and enhance business environment. The term quality means that business or organization is satisfied with the skills and knowledge, in which graduated students obtained through education. Moreover, the education system should expand further to include qualified entrepreneurs to be professors or allow academic professors to run their own businesses. These not only enhance the university and industry linkage, but also leverage the quality of professors. In addition to the short term plan should be continually maintained.

Limitation and further research

Given the purpose, the circumstance and supporting theories and methodologies, this dissertation poses a number of limitations that can be challenges for future researches. Limitation of this dissertation can be seen in the following aspects: research methodologies; scope of the research and the availability of data.

Underlying the limitation in research methodology, this dissertation has relied on patent as a proxy of firm innovation to measure the innovative competencies of manufacturing firms. As mentioned in the previous section, patents indirectly measure innovation. So they do not exactly indicate firms' innovation. Patent citation would be a better measurement approach. In addition to that, with budget constraint and unsupportive culture of answering survey, the original survey was carried out at small scale and targeting at the small group of firms attending the Techmart. Consequently, this dissertation has to rely on the World Bank for additional data for further analysis. Although, the World Bank has a rich data source, it is strictly focus on innovation but rather a broad range of data with several records that reflect firms' innovation. Moreover, in calculating patenting cost for the seven Asian countries, an assumption has been made based on Vietnamese patenting experiences. The average number of pages, the claims, the drawings of patents in the other countries may be different with the ones in Vietnam.

Another limitation must describe here is the scope of the research and the availability of data. As the research topic is quite new and unique, the availability of referential information is quite limited. Furthermore, a partial of the dissertation has covered a wide range of developing Asian countries, where information is discrete, distortion, and hindering. These weaknesses have been barriers to author to get adequate information for better analysis and interpretation.

These limitations can also be the challenges for further researches in the future. The scope of the research can be also further expanded to service firms or targeted deeper to specific fields. Furthermore, when information is available, firm innovation can also be measured by other methods, such as the turn over generated by new product or process in each firm. In despite of those limitations, this research has provided a clearer picture of innovation system in Vietnam. The finding of this research can help authorities in generating such crucial policies to helping firms moving forwards in international markets.

REFERENCES

1. Afuah 1998, Innovation Management-Strategies, Implementation and profits, Oxford University Press.

2. Alfred K. and Pierre M., Innovation and Firm Performance – Econometric Explorations of Survey Data, 2002, Palgrave.

3. Álvarez, R, Crespi, G, and Ramos, J 2002, The impact of licenses on a 'late starter' LDC: Chile in the 1990s. World Development, vol.30, issue 8, pp.1445–1460.

4. Aranda and Rata and Duarte, Innovation and firm size: an empirical study for Spanish engineering consulting companies, 2001, European Journal of Innovation Management, Vol.4, No.3.

5. Argyres, N and Silverman, B 2004, 'R&D, organization structure, and the development of corporate technological knowledge', *Strategic Management*, vol. 25, issue 8-9, pp. 929–958.

6. Article 4, Ordinance No.12 of Vietnam, 1999.

7. Baker and Mc Kenzie, 'Collection of evidence and assessment of damages regarding IP rights infringement, Building and enforcing intellectual property value', *IP value 2007*, pp. 184-187.

8. Bell, M and Pavitt, K 1993, 'Technological accumulation and industrial growth: contrasts between developed and developing countries', *Industrial and Corporate Change*, vol. 2, issue1, pp. 157–210.

9. Belussi, F 1999, Policies for the development of knowledge-intensive local production systems, Cambridge Political Economy Society, vol. 23, pp. 729-747.

10. Bezanson, K, Oldham, G and Tran, C 2000, A science technology and industry strategy for Vietnam, Industrial Policies and Research Branch, UNIDO, viewed 2 May 2009, <http://www.unido.org/fileadmin/import/20398_kbfin.pdf>.

11. Brouwer, E and Kleinknecht, A 1999, 'Innovative output and a firm's propensity to patent: An exploration of CIS micro data', *Research Policy*, vol. 28, issue 6, pp. 615-624

12. Brown E. and Ulijn J., Innovation, Entrepreneurship and Culture – The

Interaction between Technology, Progress and Economics Growth, 2004, Edward Elgar.

13.Business Software Alliance, 2010, seventh annual bsa/idc global software – 09 piracy study, Business Software Alliance, viewed 20 March 2011, < http://www.bsa.org/>

14.Casper, S and Waarden, F 2005, *Innovation and Institutions- A Multidisplinary Review of the Study of Innovation System*, Edward Elgar.

15.Chaston 1997, Small firm performance: assessing the interaction between entrepreneurial style and organizational structure, European Journal of Marketing, Vol.31, No.11/12.

16.Cobbenhagen, Successful Innovation-Towards a new theory for the Management of Small and Medium sized Enterprises, 2000, Edward Elgar.

17.Damanpour, F 1991, 'Organizational innovation: a meta-analysis of effects of determinants and moderators', *The Academy of Management Journal,* vol. 34, No. 3, pp. 555-590.

18.Davenport T. 1993, Process Innovation-Reengineering work through Information Technology, Harvard Business School Press.

19.de Rassenfosse, G and van Pottelsberghe de la Potterie, B 2009, A policy insight into the R&D-patent relationship, Research Policy, Elsevier, vol. 38(5), pages 779-792

20.de Rassenfosse, G and van Pottelsberghe de la Potterie, B 2012. On the price elasticity of demand for patents, *Oxford Bulletin of Economics and Statistics*, Department of Economics, University of Oxford, vol. 74, issue 1, pp 58-77.

21.de Rassenfosse, G and van Pottelsberghe de la Potterie, B 2010, The Role of Fees in Patent Systems: Theory and Evidence. Université Libre de Bruxelles, ECARES working paper 2010 ‑ 023.

22.De Bresson, C 1996, *Economic interdependence and innovative activity. An input-output analysis*, Edward Elgar.

23.Drahos, P 2008, 'Trust Me: Patent Offices in Developing Countries', *American Journal of Law and Medicine*, vol. 34, issue: 2-3, pp. 151-74.

24.Fagerberg, J, Srholec, M and Verspagen, B 2010, 'Innovation and economic development', In Hall, B and Rosenberge, N (ed), *Handbook of the economics of innovation*, Elsevier, pp. 833-872.

25.Ford, T and Rork, J 2010, 'Why buy what you can get for free? The effect of foreign direct investment on state patent rates', *Journal of Urban Economics*, vol. 68, pp. 72–81.

26.Foxon, T and Pearson, P 2008, 'Overcoming barriers to innovation and diffusion of cleaner technologies: some features of a sustainable innovation policy regime', *Journal of Cleaner Production*, vol.16, pp. 148-161.

27.Freeman, C 1971, 'Technology assessment and its social context', *Stadium Generale*, vol. 24, pp. 1038-1050.

28.Ginarte, J and Park, W 1997 'Determinants of patent rights: A cross-national study', *Research Policy*, vol. 26, issue 3, pp. 283-301.

29.Govindaraju, C and Wong, C 2011, 'Patenting activities by developing countries: The case of Malaysia', *World Patent Information*, vol. 33, pp. 51-57.

30.Grossman and Helpman, Innovation and Growth in the Global Economy, 1993, The MIT press.

31.GSO 2011, *Statistical yearbook of Vietnam 2010*, Statistical Publishing House, 264 p.

32.Guellec, D and van Pottelsberghe de la Potterie, B 2007, *The Economics of the European Patent System*, Oxford University Press, Oxford, 250 p.

33.Hall, B, Graham, S, Harhoff, D and Mowery, D 2004, 'Prospects for Improving U.S. Patent Quality via Postgrant Opposition', *Innovation Policy and the Economy*, National Bureau of Economic Research Inc, vol. 4, pp. 115-144 .

34.Hemphill, T 2008, 'U.S. patent policy: Crafting a 21st century national blueprint for global competitiveness', *Knowledge and Technology Policy*, vol. 21, issue 2, pp.83-96.

35.Hu, A and Jefferson, G 2009, 'A great wall of patents: What is behind China's recent patent explosion?', *Journal of Development Economics*, vol. 90, issue 1, pp. 57-68.

36.Huergo, E and Jaumandreu, J 2004, 'Firms' age, process innovation and productivity growth', *International Journal of Industrial Organization*, vol. 22, issue 4, pp. 541-559.

37. Ishihara, T 2008, 'Problems Related to Patent Enforcement in Japan, the United States and South Korea', *IIP Bulletin*, pp. 88-97.

38. Jonash R. and Sommerlatte T., The Innovation Premium-How Next Generation Companies Are Achieving Peak Performance and Profitability, 1999, Perseus Books.

39. *Journal of Law, Economics, and Organization*, vol. 15, issue 3, pp. 637-658.

40. *Journal*, vol. 14, pp. 95–112.

41. Kariodimedjo, D 2006, *Overview of IP Courses in Indonesia*, ECAP project II, viewed 15 June 2008 <http://www.ecap-project.org/>

42. Katz R., The Human Side of Managing Technological Innovation, 1997, Oxford University Press.

43. Kline, S and Rosenberg, N 1986, 'An overview of innovation. The Positive Sum Strategy: Harnessing Technology for Economic Growth', in Landau and et al (eds), *The Positive Sum Strategy*, National Academy Press, pp. 275-305.

44. Krammer, S 2009, 'Drivers of national innovation in transition: Evidence from a panel of Eastern European countries', *Research Policy*, vol. 38, issue 5, pp. 845-860.

45. Kumar, S and Ellingson, J 2007, 'Adaptive IP strategies in China: a tactical analysis', *Journal of Intellectual Capital*, vol. 8, issue 1, pp.139-158.

46. Lanjouw, J and Schankerman, M 2004, 'Patent Quality and Research Productivity: Measuring Innovation with Multiple Indicators', *The Economic Journal*, vol. 114, issue 495, pp. 441–465.

47. Leede, J, Looise, J and Alders, B 2002, 'Innovation, improvement and operations: an exploration of the management of alignment', *International Journal of Technology Management*, vol. 23, issue 4, pp. 353-368.

48. Leonard-Barton, D 1998, 'Importing and absorbing technological knowledge from outside of the firm', *Wellsprings of Knowledge: Building and Sustaining the Sources of Innovation*, Harvard Business School Press, Boston, MA.

49. Levinthal, D and March, J 1993, 'The myopia of learning', *Strategic Management*

50. Loderer, C and Waelchli U, Firm Age and Performance, 2010. Available at SSRN: http://ssrn.com/abstract=1342248 or http://dx.doi.org/10.2139/ssrn.1342248.

51. MacLeod, C, Tann, J, Andrew, J & Stein, J 2003, 'Evaluating inventive activity: the cost of nineteenth-century UK patents and the fallibility of renewal data', *The Economic History Review*, vol. 56, issue 3, pp. 537–562.

52. McMillan, J and Woodruff, C 1999, 'Dispute prevention without courts in Vietnam', *Journal of Law, Economics and Organization*, vol. 15, issue 3, pp. 637-658.

53. MOST, 2009, *Assisting enterprises for intellectual property development*, Report program CT168, Hanoi.

54. Motohashi and Yun, China's Innovation System and Growing Industry and Science Linkages, 2005.

55. Nguyen, T 2011, 'Investments and Capital issues on Science and Technology in Vietnam', *Political Science Journal*, vol. 3, pp.54-58.

56. Nicholas, T 2011, 'Cheaper patents', *Research Policy*, vol. 40, issue 2, pp. 325-339.

57. Nunnenkamp, P and Spatz, J 2004, 'Intellectual Property Rights and Foreign Direct Investment: A Disaggregated Analysis', *Review of World Economics*, vol. 140, issue 3, pp. 393-414.

58. Oxfarm International. Extortion at gate. Will Vietnam join the WTO on Pro-Development Terms? Oxfarm Briefing Paper 67. online
www.oxfam.org/eng/pdfs/bp67_Viet_%20Nam_041004.pdf

59. Park, W 2008, 'International Patent Protection: 1960-2005', *Research Policy*, vol. 37, pp. 761-766.

60. Pavitt, K 1985, 'Patent statistics as indicators of innovative activities: possibilities and problems', *Scientometrics*, vol. 7, issue 1-2, pp.77-99.

61. Peeters C and Van Pottelsberghe 2003, Measuring Innovation Competencies and Performances – A survey of large firms in Belgium, 2003, ULB-CEB working paper 04-005.

62. Peeters, C and van Pottelsberghe de la Potterie, B 2006, 'Innovation strategy and the patenting behavior of firms', *Journal of Evolutionary Economics*, vol. 16, issue 1, pp. 109-135.

63. Phan, V 2009, 'Vietnam', In Goldstein, P and Straus, J (ed), *Intellectual Property in Asia - Law, Economics, History and Politics - MPI studies on intellectual property, competition and tax law*, Springer, vol. 9, pp. 331-357.

64. Rahmounia, M, Ayadia, M and Yildizoglub, M 2010, 'Characteristics of innovating firms in Tunisia: The essential role of external knowledge sources', *Structural Change and Economic Dynamics*, vol. 21, pp.181–196.

65. Regan and Ghobadian, Innovation in SMEs: the impact of strategic orientation and environmental perceptions, 2005, International Journal of Productivity and Performance Management Vol.54. No.2.

66. Sanidas, Organizational Innovation and Economic Growth, 2005, Edward Elgar Publishing Inc.

67. Schumpeter, J 1934, *The Theory of Economic Development*, Cambride: Harvard University Press. (New York: Oxford University Press, 1961).

68. Sorg, J 2009, 'Thailand', In Goldstein, P and Straus, J (ed), *Intellectual Property in Asia - Law, Economics, History and Politics - MPI studies on intellectual property, competition and tax law*, Springer, vol. 9, pp. 303-330.

69. Spoo R. and Dao, T 2010, *Intellectual property and Vietnam's higher education system, Reforming higher education in Vietnam: challenges and priorities*, Higher education dynamic, vol. 29, 232p.

70. Steer, L and Sen, K 2010, 'Formal and Informal Institutions in a Transition Economy: The Case of Vietnam', *World Development*, vol. 38, issue 11, pp. 1603-1615.

71. Tidd, John and Pavitt, Managing Innovation-Integrating Technological, Market and Organizational Change, 2001, John Wiley & Sons.

72. Tran T., Daim T., Kocaoglu D., 2011, 'Comparative study on Government Technology Transfer to Industry in the US and Vietnam', *Technology in Society*, Vol 33, No 1, pp 84-93.

73. Tran, C 2006, 'Universities as Drivers of the Urban Economies in Asia: The Case of Vietnam', *World Bank Policy Research*, Working Paper No. 3949.

74. Tran, C and Nguyen, H 2011, 'Vietnam: Current Debates on the Transformation of Academic Institutions', IN: Göransson, B and Brundenius, C (Ed), *University in Transition: Insight and Innovation in International Development*, pp. 119-142, DOI: 10.1007/978-1-4419-7509-6_7.

75. Trott, P 1998, 'Innovation Management: Introduction', *Innovation Management and New Product Development*, Prentice Hall, 535 p.

76. UNCTAD, FDI,
http://stats.unctad.org/FDI/TableViewer/tableView.aspx?ReportId=3084 (Accessed May 2010).

77. USTR, 2010, 2010 special 301 report, available at http://www.ustr.gov/webfm_send/1906

78. Utterback, J and Abernathy, W 1975, 'A dynamic model of process and product innovation', *Omega*, vol.3 issue 6, pp. 639–656.

79. van Pottelsberghe, de la Potterie B 2011, 'The quality factor in patent systems', *Industrial and Corporate Change*, Oxford University Press, vol. 20(6), pp. 1755-1793

80. van Pottelsberghe, de la Potterie B and François, D 2009, 'The Cost Factor in Patent Systems', *Journal of Industry, Competition and Trade*, vol. 9, issue 4, pp. 329-355.

81. van Pottelsberghe, de la Potterie B and Mejer, M 2010, 'The London agreement and the cost of patenting in Europe', *European Journal of Law and Economics*, vol. 29, issue 2, pp. 211-237.

82. Varsakelis, C 2001, 'The impact of patent protection, economy openness and national culture on R&D investment: a cross-country empirical investigation', *Research Policy*, Elsevier, vol. 30, issue 7, pp. 1059-1068.

83. Vu N, Le L and Nguyen A, 2010, Factors influence to the development of handicraft village – case of Van Phuc silk village, Economic development journal, Vietnam.

84. Vu T. Yen, Nguyen T. Tu and Nguyen V. Hai 2010, 'Handling industrial design infringements, untouched problems', *Journal of Scientific Activity*, Vol.1.

85. Wagner and Hansen 2005, Innovation in large versus small companies: insights from the US wood products industry, Management Decision, Vol.43.

86. WEF, 2010, the Global Competitiveness Report 2010-2011, available at http://www.weforum.org/reports

87. WIPO, http://www.wipo.int/ipstats/en/statistics/patents/ (Accessed May 2010)

88. World Bank, 2008, World Bank, http://data.worldbank.org/ (Accessed May 2010)

89. World Bank, 2009, World Bank, http://data.worldbank.org/ (Accessed May 2010)

90. Yoon, H and Tran, N. Kien, 2011, 'Vietnam's intellectual property landscape from a regional perspective', *International Area Studies Review*, vol. 14, issue1, pp. 73-104.

APPENDIX 1. Questionnaire

Characteristics of firms

1. Year of establishment
2. Size (No. of employees)
3. Legal status (SOE, Private, Foreign)
4. Business field
5. Sale/profit/State budget
6. Having at least 1 patent (Y/N)

Innovative culture

1. Does the firm organize any contest annually for new ideas or new solutions (Y/N)
2. Does the firm provide reward (monetary/ salary leverage/ certification) for innovative ideas or solution? (Y/N)
3. Does the firm support employees for further education (allow time to study/ pay partial tuition fee/ pay full tuition fee) (Y/N)
4. Friendly working environment (sharing of ideas/information) (Likert scale 1-5)
5. Does the firm participate in the program 168 (Y/N)

External source for ideas

1. Does the firm collaborate with Customer/ Supplier; (Y/N)
2. Does the firm collaborate with Competitor; (Y/N)
3. Does the firm collaborate with University's personnel (Y/N)
4. Does the firm use Patent library for knowledge generation (Likert scale 1-5)

Firm's ability in implementing new ideas

1. Percentage of employee having a degree (%)
2. Does the firm purchase high tech equipment (Y/N)
3. Does the firm have accessibility to external fund for R&D (Y/N)

APPENDIX Ia

WORLD BANK DATA SET VARIABLES

Variable	Variable description	Sample size	Coding
Characteristics of Firms			
Age	Years of establishment (calculating to year 2009)	520	
Size	Size of firms (OECD**)	521	Large:3; Medium:2: Small: 1
LegalBType	Legal Business Type (*)	521	Private: 1; Foreign: 2; SOE: 3
TechOECD	Technology advancement	521	HT & MH:1; ML & LT: 0
Ability to Implement new ideas			
Certification	Having or acquiring international certifications (ISO)? (Y/N)	520	(Y/N); Y:1; N:0
TechLicense	Acquiring technology licensing? (Y/N)	521	Y:1; N:0
Eeducation	Average employee education (High education(HE) >13 years of study)	519	HE:1; Low Education (LE):0
Training	Having formal training? (Y/N)	520	Y:1; N:0
Barrier to Innovation			
CourtFair	Court system is fair (Likert:1-4)	337	4 coded as 1; 1,2,3 coded as 0
Innovative Output			
Patent	Having at least 1 patent? (Y/N)	521	Y:1; N:0

* *A classification of technology advancement based on Oslo manual (OECD, 1997), technology advancement is classified into High tech (HT); Medium high tech (MH); Medium low tech (ML); and low tech (LT).*

** *Legal businesses are clarified as: Private; Foreign; State Owned Enterprise (SOE); The term Foreign includes Foreign Joint Venture, which has more than or equal to 20% of shares in a company.*

APPENDIX Ib

SURVEY DATA SET VARIABLES

Variable	Variable description	Sample size	Coding
Characteristics of Firms			
Age	Years of establishment (calculating to year 2009)	64	Number
EmployeeC	Number of employees in 2009	64	Number
LegalBType	Legal Business Type (*)	64	Private: 1; Foreign: 2; SOE: 3
Size	Size of firms (OECD**)	64	Large:3; Medium:2: Small: 1
TechOECD	Technology advancement	64	HT & MH:1; ML & LT: 0
Firms Innovative culture			
InnoCont	Innovation Contest (Y/N)	64	Y:1; N:0
Reward	*Reward (Y/N), which is comprised of Monetary; SalInc; and Recognition.*	64	Y:1 for 2 or more selections; N:0 otherwise
Monetary	Monetary (Y/N)	64	Y:1; N:0
SalInc	Increase in salary (Y/N)	64	Y:1; N:0
Recognition	Certificate of Recognition (Y/N)	64	Y:1; N:0
StudyOpp	*StudyOpp (Y/N), which is comprised of Timestudy; PartTuition; and FullTuition.*	64	Y:1 for 2 or more selections; N:0 otherwise
TimeStudy	Time to Study (Y/N)	64	Y:1; N:0
PartTuition	Partial Tuition (Y/N)	64	Y:1; N:0
FullTuition	Full Tuition (Y/N)	64	Y:1; N:0

119

WorkEnv	Friendly Working Environment (Likert:1-5)	64	4, 5 coded as 1; 1,2,3 coded as 0
CT168	Firm participation in CT168? (Y/N)	64	Y:1; N:0

External sources of ideas

Collaboration	*Collaboration (Y/N), which is comprised of Competitor; Supplier; and UniPersonnel.*	64	Y:1 for 2 or more selections; N:0 otherwise
Competitor	Collaboration with Competitor? (Y/N)	64	Y:1; N:0
Supplier	Collaboration with Supplier (Y/N)	64	Y:1; N:0
UniPersonnel	Collaboration with Universities' personnel (Y/N)	64	Y:1; N:0
Patent Doc	Use patent document for new ideas (Likert:1-5)	64	4, 5 coded as 1; 1,2,3 coded as 0

Firm's ability in implementing new ideas

Eeducation	Percentage of Employee having a degree? (%)	64	
TechLicense	Acquiring technology licensing in the last 5 years? (Y/N)	64	Y:1; N:0
FundingS	Accession to funding source (Y/N)	64	Y:1; N:0
SalePEmp	Sale per employee	64	

Firms Innovative outputs

Patent	Having at least 1 Patent in last 10 years? (Y/N)	64	Y:1; N:0

* *A classification of technology advancement based on Oslo manual (OECD, 1997), technology advancement is classified into High tech (HT); Medium high tech (MH); Medium low tech (ML); and low tech (LT).*

** *Legal businesses are clarified as: Private; Foreign; State Owned Enterprise (SOE); The term Foreign includes Foreign Joint Venture, which has more than or equal to 20% of shares in a company.*

APPENDIX 2. Patents filed at NPO in the period of 1991-2008

Patent Office	Applicant Type	1991	1992	1993	1994	1995	1996	1997	1998	1999
	Resident	7,372	10,022	12,084	11,191	10,011	11,628	12,672	13,751	15,626
	Non-Resident	4,051	4,387	7,534	7,876	8,688	11,114	12,102	33,645	34,418
China	Total	11,423	14,409	19,618	19,067	18,699	22,742	24,774	47,396	50,044
	Resident	34	67	38	29	61	40	79	93	152
	Non-Resident	1,280	3,905	2,031	2,307	2,813	4,027	3,939	1,753	2,784
Indonesia	Total	1,314	3,972	2,069	2,336	2,874	4,067	4,018	1,846	2,936
	Resident	106	151	198	223	185	221	179	193	218
Malaysia	Non- Resident	2,321	2,260	2,684	3,364	3,992	5,354	6,278	5,770	5,624
	Total	2,427	2,411	2,882	3,587	4,177	5,575	6,457	5,963	5,842
	Resident	147	133	178	181	169	163	125	163	144
	Non-Resident	1,774	1,687	1,860	1,965	2,207	2,634	3,440	3,280	3,217
Philippines	Total	1,921	1,820	2,038	2,146	2,376	2,797	3,565	3,443	3,361
	Resident					145	224	288	311	374
Singapore	Non- Resident					2,412	12,357	6,048	6,367	6,679
	Total					2,557	12,581	6,336	6,678	7,053
	Resident	80	67	110	150	145	203	246	479	738
	Non-Resident	1,907	1,906	2,353	2,816	3,387	4,355	5,148	4,592	4,438
Thailand	Total	1,987	1,973	2,463	2,966	3,532	4,558	5,394	5,071	5,176
	Resident	37	34	32	22	23	37	30	25	37
	Non- Resident	25	49	193	270	659	929	1,234	1,080	1,105
Viet Nam	Total	62	83	225	292	682	966	1,264	1,105	1,142
	Resident	87,955	92,425	99,955	107,233	123,962	106,892	119,214	134,733	149,251
	Non- Resident	84,160	90,922	84,241	95,522	104,180	105,054	101,282	102,246	116,512
US	Total	172,115	183,347	184,196	202,755	228,142	211,946	220,496	236,979	265,763

Patent Office	Applicant Type	2000	2001	2002	2003	2004	2005	2006	2007	2008
	Resident	25,346	30,038	39,806	56,769	65,786	93,485	122,318	153,060	194,579
	Non-Resident	26,560	33,412	40,426	48,548	64,598	79,842	88,183	92,101	95,259
China	Total	51,906	63,450	80,232	105,317	130,384	173,327	210,501	245,161	289,838
	Resident	156	208	228	201	226	234	282	279	375
	Non-Resident	3,733	3,714	3,609	3,099	3,441	4,069	4,324	4,850	4,747
Indonesia	Total	3,889	3,922	3,837	3,300	3,667	4,303	4,606	5,129	5,122
	Resident	206	271	322	376	522	522	531	670	864
Malaysia	Non-Resident	6,021	5,663	4,615	4,686	4,920	5,764	4,269	1,702	4,539
	Total	6,227	5,934	4,937	5,062	5,442	6,286	4,800	2,372	5,403
	Resident	154	135	149	141	158	210	223	225	216
	Non-Resident	3,482	2,470	705	1,732	2,538	2,141	3,034	3,248	3,095
Philippines	Total	3,636	2,605	854	1,873	2,696	2,351	3,257	3,473	3,311
	Resident	516	523	624	626	641	569	626	696	793
Singapore	Non-Resident	7,720	8,133	7,575	7,280	7,944	8,036	8,537	9,255	8,899
	Total	8,236	8,656	8,199	7,906	8,585	8,605	9,163	9,951	9,692
	Resident	561	534	615	802	819	891	1,040	945	802
	Non-Resident	4,488	4,798	3,874	4,329	4,554	5,449	5,221	5,873	5,939
Thailand	Total	5,049	5,332	4,489	5,131	5,373	6,340	6,261	6,818	6,741
	Resident	34	52	69	78	103	180	196	219	204
	Non-Resident	1,210	1,234	1,142	1,097	1,328	1,767	1,970	2,641	2,995
Viet Nam	Total	1,244	1,286	1,211	1,175	1,431	1,947	2,166	2,860	3,199
	Resident	164,795	177,513	184,245	188,941	189,536	207,867	221,784	241,347	231,588
	Non-Resident	131,100	148,958	150,200	153,500	167,407	182,866	204,182	214,807	224,733
US	Total	295,895	326,471	334,445	342,441	356,943	390,733	425,966	456,154	456,321

121

APPENDIX 3.   Patenting cost in the developing ASEAN countries

Country	Indonesia	Malaysia	Philippines	Singapore	Thailand	Vietnam	
Currency	Rupiah (thousand)	Ringgit	Peso	Singapore Dollar	Baht	Dong (thousand)	
Filing	575	290	3,600	160		1,000 1 claim	150
Exceeding page			30 pages / 30			5 pages	10
Exceeding claim	10 claims / 40	10 claims	20 5 claims / 300				
Publication	250		5550			500	100
Publication of drawing						>1 drawing	50
Search	local 250					1 claim	100
Examination	substantive 2,000	1,100	Search & Exam 3500	2600		500 1 claim	350
Granting				170 or 200+s			100
Administrative cost							
Annual renewal fee							
1st year	700+50 * AC	290					250
2nd year	700+50 * AC	290					250
3rd year	700+50 * AC	360					400
4th year	700+50 * AC	420					400
5th year	1000+100 * AC	490	2700	160	2,000		650
6th year	1500+150 * AC	560	3600	160	4,000		650
7th year	2000+200 * AC	640	4500	160	6,000		1,000
8th year	2000+200 * AC	690	5400	270	8,000		1,000
9th year	2500+250 * AC	760	7200	270	10,000		1,500
10th year	3500+250 * AC	820	9000	270	12,000		1,500
11th year	5000+250 * AC	890	11,600	350	14,000		2,100
12th year	5000+250 * AC	940	14,400	350	16,000		2,100
13th year	5000+250 * AC	1,100	17,000	350	18,000		2,100
14th year	5000+250 * AC	1,250	20,700	450	20,000		2,750
15th year	5000+250 * AC	1,350	24,300	450	30,000		2,750
16th year	5000+250 * AC	1,660	27,800	450	40,000		2,750
17th year	5000+250 * AC	1,900	31,400	550	50,000		3,500
18th year	5000+250 * AC	2,200	37,700	550	60,000		3,500
19th year	5000+250 * AC	2,500	45,300	550	70,000		3,500
20th year	5000+250 * AC	2,700	54,300	650	80,000		3,500

Philippines: 350 is required to be paid for each exceeding claim

Thailand: Inventor can pay a lump sum of 400000 for a total 20 year protection

AC: Additional exceeding claim; **s**: if a patent has more than 25 claim, then the granting cost = 200+20* exceeding claims.

APPENDIX 4. Authorized Administrative Fines

Authority	Year 1999 (Ordinance No. 12/1999) Major authorized acts	Max fine (monetary) 1USD=11,900 VND	Year 2006 (Ordinance No. 106/2006) Major authorized acts	Max fine (monetary) 1USD=15,900 VND	Year 2010 (Ordinance No. 97/2010) Major authorized acts	Max fine (monetary) 1USD=18,500 VND
People committees						
Director of a district and equivalent	• warn; fine; confiscate (evidences' value<100millions VND–8,400USD); • withdraw business license (district issued) temporarily or permanently. • order to compensate • order to remove infringed parts • destroy infringed products (poor quality, or affect human health)	10 millions VND (840 USD)	• warn; fine; confiscate • withdraw business license (province or district issued) • order to compensate • order to remove infringed parts • destroy infringed products (poor quality, or affect human health)	20 millions VND (1,258USD)	• warn; fine; confiscate. • withdraw business license (province or district issued) • order to compensate • order to remove infringed parts • destroy infringed products (poor quality, or affect human health)	30 millions VND (1,622 USD)
Director of province or equivalent	• warn; fine; confiscate. • withdraw business license (province or district issued) temporarily or permanently. • order to compensate • order to remove infringed parts • destroy infringed products (poor quality, or affect human health)	100 millions VND (8,400USD)	• warn; fine; confiscate. • withdraw authorized license (province or district issued) • suspend business license (province or district issued) temporarily • order to compensate • order to remove	5 times of the value of infringed products.	• warn; fine; confiscate. • withdraw business license (province or district issued) temporarily or permanently. • order to compensate • order to remove infringed parts • destroy infringed products (poor quality, or affect human	500 millions VND (27,023 USD)

Inspectorate Department of Science and Technology (IDST)

		infringed parts; destroy infringed products (poor quality, or affect human health)				health)
Inspector of IDST	200,000 VND (17 USD)	warn; fine; confiscate (evidences' value<500,000 VND~42USD); order to compensate; order to remove infringed parts; destroy infringed products (poor quality, or affect human health)	200,000 VND (12.5 USD)	warn; fine; confiscate (evidences' value< 2,000,000 VND~ 126 USD); order to compensate; order to remove infringed parts; destroy infringed products (poor quality, or affect human health)	2 millions VND (108 USD)	warn; fine; confiscate order to remove infringed parts; destroy infringed products (poor quality, or affect human health)
Chief inspector of IDST (Province/City)	10 millions VND (840 USD)	warn; fine; confiscate (evidences' value<100millions VND~8,400USD); withdraw authorized license (province, district issued) temporarily or permanently. order to compensate; order to remove infringed parts; destroy infringed products (poor quality, or affect human health)	20 millions VND (1.258 USD)	warn; fine; confiscate withdraw authorized license (province, district issued) temporarily or permanently. order to compensate; order to remove infringed parts; destroy infringed products (poor quality, or affect human health)	30 millions VND (1,622 USD)	warn; fine; confiscate. withdraw authorized license (province, district issued) temporarily withdraw business license (province, district issued) up to 3 months. order to compensate; order to remove infringed parts; destroy infringed products (poor quality, or affect human health)

Chief inspector of IDST (Ministry)	• warn; fine; confiscate • withdraw authorized license temporarily or permanently. • order to compensate • order to remove infringed parts • destroy infringed products (poor quality,or affect human health)	20 millions VND (1,680USD)	warn; fine; confiscate 5 times of the value of infringed products. • withdraw authorized license temporarily or permanently. • order to compensate • order to remove infringed parts • destroy infringed products (poor quality,or affect human health)	• warn; fine; confiscate. • withdraw authorized license (province, district issued) temporarily • withdraw business license up to 6 months. • order to compensate • order to remove infringed parts • destroy infringed products (poor quality,or affect human health)	500 millions VND (27,023 USD)
Inspectorate Department of Information and Telecommunication (IDIT)					
Inspector of IDIT (Ministry/ Province/ City)	not defined		not defined	• warn; fine; confiscate (evidences' value< 2 millions VND~ 108 millions USD);	
Chief inspector of IDIT (Province/City)	not defined		not defined	• warn; fine; confiscate. • withdraw authorized license (province, district issued) up to 3 months.	30 millions VND (1,622 USD)
Chief inspector of IDIT (Ministry)	not defined		not defined	• warn; fine; confiscate. • withdraw authorized license (province, district issued) up to 6 months.	70 millions VND (3,784 USD)
Market Control Management (MCM)					
Team leader MCM	• warn; fine; confiscate (evidences' value<30millions VND~ 1,887 USD);	5 millions VND (315 USD)		• warn; fine; confiscate (evidences' value<30millions VND~ 1,622 USD);	5 millions VND (270 USD)

Head of MCM (District)	• warn; fine; confiscate • withdraw authorized license • order to compensate • order to remove infringed parts • destroy infringed products (poor quality, or affect human health)	10 millions VND (USD)	• warn; fine; confiscate • withdraw authorized license • order to compensate • order to remove infringed parts • destroy infringed products (poor quality, or affect human health)	20 millions VND (1,258 USD)	• withdraw authorized license • order to compensate • order to remove infringed parts • destroy infringed products (poor quality, or affect human health)	20 millions VND (1,080 USD)
Chief of MCM (Province)	• warn; fine; confiscate • withdraw authorized license • order to compensate • order to remove infringed parts • destroy infringed products (poor quality, or affect human health)	20 millions VND (USD)	• warn; fine; confiscate • withdraw authorized license • order to compensate • order to remove infringed parts • destroy infringed products (poor quality, or affect human health)	70 millions VND (4,402USD)	• warn; fine; confiscate • withdraw authorized license • order to compensate • order to remove infringed parts • destroy infringed products (poor quality, or affect human health)	70 millions VND (3,784 USD)
Police						
Chief of police (District); Head department of economic police	warn; fine; confiscate (evidences)	2 millions VND (168 USD)	warn; fine; confiscate (evidences) – applicable to Head department of economic police	10 millions VND (629 USD) - applicable to Head department of	warn; fine; confiscate (evidences) – this also extended to chief of police (border control)	10 millions VND (540 USD) - this also extended to chief of police

	(Province)		(Province)	economic police (Province)		(border control)
Chief of police (Province); Director of Directorate of economic police	warn; fine; confiscate (evidences)	20 millions VND (1,680 USD)	not defined	not defined	warn; fine; confiscate (evidences); order to compensate; order to remove infringed parts; destroy infringed products (poor quality, or affect human health) (applicable to chief police of province)	30 millions VND (1,622 USD) – (applicable to chief police of province)
Director of Crime Investigation Department	not defined		warn; fine; confiscate (evidences); order to compensate; order to remove infringed parts; destroy infringed products (poor quality, or affect human health)	100 millions VND (6,290 USD)	warn; fine; confiscate; order to compensate; order to remove infringed parts; destroy infringed products (poor quality, or affect human health)	500 millions VND (27,023 USD)
Custom office						
Team leader of Custom office (border control)	warn; fine; confiscate (evidences)' value up to 20 millions VND~1,680 USD)	2 millions VND (168 USD)			warn; fine	5 millions VND (270 USD)
Head of Custom office (border control); Head of Inspector of Custom office (province) From 2010 the			warn; fine; confiscate (evidences)' value up to 20 millions VND (1,258 USD) applicable to Head of control unit – Custom	10 millions VND (629 USD) applicable to Head of control unit – Custom office (province); Head of	warn; fine; confiscate withdraw authorized license	20 millions VND (1,080 USD)

Authority	office (province); Head of custom office (district)	custom office (district)			
following officers are on duty: (Head of anti-smuggling team; Head of control team; Head of squadron)					
Chief of Custom office (province); **From 2010 the following officers are on duty**: Chief of smuggling crime investigation department; Chief of post-clearance control department	20 millions VND (1,680 USD) • warn; fine; confiscate • withdraw authorized license • order to remove infringed parts • destroy infringed products (poor quality, or affect human health)	20 millions VND (1,258 USD) • warn; fine; confiscate • withdraw authorized license • order to compensate • order to remove infringed parts • destroy infringed products (poor quality, or affect human health)	70 millions VND (3,784 USD) • warn; fine; confiscate • withdraw authorized license • order to compensate • order to remove infringed parts • destroy infringed products (poor quality, or affect human health)		
Unfair competition Department					
Director of unfair competition department	not defined	not defined	70 millions VND (3,784 USD) • warn; fine; confiscate • withdraw authorized license • order to compensate • order to remove infringed parts • destroy infringed products (poor quality, or affect human health)		

APPENDIX 5. Patent and Utility Solutions' Infringement Cases

Case	Description	IP Owner /Size	IP Infringer /Size	Start date /End date /Duration (days)	Types of settlement	USD/ VND	Fine Millions VND	Fine USD	Extra penalty
GIVI SRL><DucMinh Locking system for Motorbike's carrying case. Registration No. 4916(5/5/2005)	IDST & Economics Police investigated and found 96 infringed lock sets	Foreign /Large	Domestic /Small	9-6-2008 /11-11-2008 /155	Administration	16,950	4.75	280	Discarded 96 lock sets
TienThinh><LocTruong Xuan Rolling door system. Registration No. 551(11-7-2006)	IDST investigated and found 2327kg of infringed rolling door parts	Domestic /Small	Domestic /Small	25-6-2009 /14-10-2009 /111	Administration				No penalty, since two parties reached an agreement.
TienThinh><TienLuong Rolling door system. Registration No. 551(11-7-2006)	IDST investigated and found 168kg of infringed rolling door parts	Domestic/ Small	Domestic /Small	25-6-2009 /14-9-2009 /81	Administration	17,833	8.4	471	Removed 471 infringed parts
HungPhuThanh><CuaC hauUc Shaped aluminum frame. Registration No. 774	IDST investigated and found 8 door sets and 590kg of frames of infringed products	Domestic /Small	Domestic /Small	21-8-2009 /10-3-2010 /201	Administration	19,100	55.46	2,904	Removed 2,904 infringed parts
HoangThinh><VietMy Registration No. 319(20/12/2002)	Hoang Thinh sued VietMy to a civil court for infringement of his registered brick making system.	Domestic /Small	Domestic /Small	27-3-2003 /18-7-2010 /2,670	Civil court	19,095	351	18,382	
Thanh Dong><NgocThanh	Thanh Dong sued Ngoc Thanh to a civil court for infringement of his protected curtain system.	Domestic /Small	Domestic /Small	28-11-2006 /25-11-2009 /1,093	Civil court	17,886	306	17,108	

APPENDIX 6. Industrial Designs' Infringement Cases

Case	Description	IP Owner /Size	IP Infringer /Size	Start date /End date /Duration (days)	Types of settlement	USD/ VND	Fine Millions VND	Fine USD	Extra penalty
Honda><TanHoaLoi Registration No. 4306, 5752, 7388, 7613	IDST investigated and found infringed plastic parts	Foreign /Large	Domestic /Small	7-10-2005 /19-10-2005 /12	Administration	15,746	15	953	confiscated 1097 infringed plastic parts
Honda><TrungThanh Registration No. 4306, 5752, 7388, 7613	IDST investigated and found infringed plastic parts	Foreign /Large	Domestic /Small	19-10-2005 /31-10-2005 /12	Administration	15,746	15	953	
Honda><PhuongDong Registration No. 4306, 8924, 7388, 9032, 10472, 10715.	IDST and Economics Police found 10 completed motorbikes and 1133 parts infringed Honda's registration.	Foreign /Large	Domestic /Small	1-7-2008 /25-7-2008 /24	Administration	16,8	79,2	4,714	1133 infringed parts were discarded.
Honda><TruongNgoc Registration No. 4306, 8924, 7388, 9032, 10472, 10715.	IDST and Economics Police found infringed parts in 160 completed motorbikes and 536 infringed parts.	Foreign /Large	Domestic /Small	19-12-2007 /14-1-2008 /26	Administration	15,984	100	6,256	self discarded infringed parts
VanHoa><LaoCaiTourism Registration No. 9387	IDST found 562 bottles of ShanLung wines infringed the protected industrial design of VanHoa.	Domestic /Small	Domestic /Small	24-5-2007 /5-7-2007 /42	Administration	16,134	2.351	146	
LuaViet>< LuaVietNam Registration No. 7865	IDST found 300 door sets and 60 completed coal stove having door sets infringed the registered industrial design of Lua Viet.	Domestic /Small	Domestic /Small	23-11-2006 /6-2-2007 /75	Administration				300 doors and 90 coal stoves were ordered to destroy
TonSatThep>< Hoang Anh Registration No. 12406	IDST found 4250 "ke chong bao" infringed the registered industrial design of TonSatThep.	Domestic /Small	Domestic /Small	30-10-2008 /14-12-2008 /45					destroyed 4200 sets
INAX><SuTaySon Registration No. 6380	IDST found 226 toilet sets infringed the registered industrial design of INAX	Foreign /*	Domestic /*	11-6-2009 /19-8-2009 /69	Administration	17,817	49.19	2,761	Infringed goods Not for sales

BienHoa><VietNam-DaiLoan Registration No. 3946	IDST found VietNam-DaiLoan infringed the registered industrial design of BienHoa.	Domestic /*	JointVenture */ /*	8-6-2004 */	Administration	15,746	5	318
DuyLoi><PBC Co. (Pacific Brokerage Company)	DuyLoi registered its industrial design for a hammock at NOIP and its designed was filed on the 23-3-2000. Johnson Miki filed its hammock for industrial design protection at JPO in April 2001. Johnson Miki transferred his ownership to PBC. PBC filed a law suit against Duy Loi.	Domestic /Small	Foreign /Medium	1-8-2002 /1-5-2003	/273 Civil court			
DuyLoi><C.S.W (Chung Sen Wu)	DuyLoi registered its industrial design for a hammock at NOIP and its designed was filed on the 23-3-2000. C.S.W filed for a protection of its hammock at USPTO on the 15-8-2001 and granted on the 22-10-2002. In 2003, Duy Loi received an warning not to sell his hammocks in US market due to infringement of C.S.W hammock. Duy Loi asked Pham and Associate law firm to file a law suit against C.S.W on 29-9-2004.	Domestic /Small	Foreign /Small	29-9-2004 /19-9-2005	/355 Civil court			

* missing value

APPENDIX 7. Trademarks' Infringement Cases

Case	Description	IP Owner /Size	IP Infringer /Size	Start date /End date /Duration (days)	Types of settlement	USD/ VND	Fine Million s VND	Fine USD	Extra penalty
Perfetti Van MelleSPA >< TienThanhPhat Registration No. 31426	Perfetti Van MelleSPA consulted with Economics police and IDST to investigate the trademark infringement of TienThanhPhat. At the time of the investigation, IDST and polices found 240kg of candies and 6 roles of plastic bags and 50 empty boxes	Foreign /Large	Domestic /Small	25-1-2010 /8-2-2010 /14	Administration	18,479	4.8	260	discarded all infringed signs
APEX-NTP >< VietCuong Registration No.68206	Economics police and IDST investigated VietCuong and found 672kg of saw blade bearing the infringed trademarks of NTP.	Domestic /Small	Domestic /Small	14-11-2008 /25-11-2008 /11	Administration	16,975	28.224	1,663	discarded all infringed goods
Pepsi >< NuocTinhKhietVN Registration No. 99173	Economics police and IDST investigated NuocTinhKhietVN and found this company was producing 648 bottles (1.5l) and 624 bottles (0.5l) bearing the marks AQUASTYPE, which is infringed with the protected mark - AQUAFINA.	Foreign /Large	Domestic /Small	29-7-2008 /31-7-2008 /2	Administration	16,790	2.4	143	discarded all infringed signs
HiepHung >< HoangGia Registration No. 28838	Economics police and IDST investigated Hoang Gia and found 40.000 Snack packs and 18.000 plastic bags printed with logos and marks, which infringed with the protected marks.	Domestic /Small	Domestic /Small	29-8-2006 /9-10-2006 /41	Administration	15,983	7	438	discarded all infringed signs; empty bags
Cisco >< OIC Registration No. 13432	Economics police and IDST investigated OIC and found 52 networking devices with logos and marks, which infringed with the protected marks.	Foreign /Large	Domestic /Small	1-11-2007 /23-11-2007 /22	Administration	16,052	100	6,230	confiscated
Cisco Cisco >< AIT Registration No. 13432	Economics police and IDST investigated AIT and found 11 network devices with logos and marks, which infringed with the protected marks.	Foreign /Large	Domestic /Small	1-11-2007 /19-12-2007 /48	Administration	16,055	91.319	5,688	confiscated

Name / Registration	Description	Party 1	Party 2	Dates	Authority			Result
Danone>‹Danon Registration No. 228184	Danone trademark was granted for international protection for foods, candies... etc. "Dan On" company was granted for its establishment by authority of BinhDuong Province. This company used "Danon" as its trademark for trading foods and agricultural products...etc.	Foreign /Large	Domestic /Small	4-6-2008 /27-6-2008 /23	Administration			discarded all printed danon signs
Nam Yung>‹Gia Huy Registration No. 33216	IDST found that Gia Huy had been trading 400 lighting products bearing the mark "Eagleye & picture", that was infringed the protected mark of Nam Yung.	Foreign /Large	Domestic /Small	17-11-2008 /31-12-2008 /44	Administration	17,486	6,089	348 confiscated
Sawafuji>‹UuThe Registration No. 58168	Economic police and IDST found Uu The Co. 92 electric power generators bearing the mark Elemax, which was registered for protection under Sawafuji Electric Co. Uu The has not been authorised by Sawafuji.	Foreign /Large	Domestic /Small	6-12-2007 /20-12-2007 /14	Administration	16,053	100	6,229 reexported
Mega Lifecenses>‹ DuocHoanKiem Registration No. 79641	IDST found that DuocHoanKiem had been selling Vitamine E bearing the mark "ENAT Plus", which infringed the protected mark "ENAT 400".	Foreign /Large	Domestic /Small	3-7-2009 /31-8-2009 /59	Administration			warned
GiengDayQuangNinh >‹ HaKhau Registration No. 20376, 20423	IDST found that HaKhau had produced ceramic bearing the marks, which were nearly identical to the registered trademark of GiengDayQuangNinh. In the inspection, IDST found a huge value of infringing ceramic products.	Domestic /Small	Domestic /Small	23-12-2006 /30-7-2007 /219	Administration	16,143	100	6,195 signs infringed
HungThinh>‹ HongThinh	Hung Thinh sued Hong Thinh to BinhDuong Provincial court for using trademark for its fish source products, that might cause misleading to customers.	Domestic /Small	Domestic /Small	30-10-2007 /23-5-2008 /206	Civil court			Forbidden to use tradename

Name / Registration	Description			Dates	Authority				Action
ATLASBX>< DAISUNG Registration No.21471	IDST found that DAISUNG had used trademark "HANKOOK" in its products that infringed the protected trademark of ATLASBX. At the time of the inspection, IDST found 1385 battery containers and 2 netprinting frames and boxes having the name HANKOOK in DAISUNG	Foreign /Large	Domestic /Small	25-9-2009 /5-10-2009 /10	Administration	17,845	23	1,289	Product injunction and compelled
KRONES AG><ADI Registration No.739368	IDST found 146 leaflets, 07 boxes of cards and 17kg of envelopes bearing the registered trademark of KRONES AG.	Foreign /Large	Domestic /Small	13-5-2009 /21-7-2009 /69	Administration	17,812	10	561	Product injunction and compelled
LaoCaiTourism>< VanHoa Registration No.46828	IDST found 7980 bottles of vodka and 2000 sets of label bearing "SHAN LUNG" protected trademark of LaoCaiTourism at VanHoa's warehouse.	Domestic /Small	Domestic /Small	19-7-2006 /22-8-2006 /34	Administration				Warned and requested to stop
Husqvarna><KimHun g Registration No.978393	IDST found KimHung selling two chain-saws bearing the trademark Husqvarna. KimHung was not an authorised agency of Husqvarna.	Foreign /Large	Domestic /Small	11-6-2009 /24-6-2009 /13	Administration	17,801	2.4	1352 chain-saw	Confiscated
Nestle><NamPhuong Registration No.494937, 554392	IDST found 30 boxes of Candy bearing the protected trademark "Carmilo and Figure" of Nestle in NamPhuong's warehouse.	Foreign /Large	Domestic /Small	20-11-2008 /20-1-2009 /61	Administration	17,482	1.8	103 boxes	Removed infringed figures and boxes
YENHUONG>< ThanhBinh Registration No.39173	IDST found ThanhBinh was printing and sticking protected trademark of YENHUONG in its products.	Domestic /Small	Domestic /Small	9-6-2006 /28-7-2006 /49	Administration	15.983	6	375 figures	Removed infringed figures

LOUIS VUITTON>< (1) Shop 57C (Thanh Huyền) (2) Shop Lan Phương (3) Leather Shop 1 (4) Leather Shop 2 (5) Toma Shop (6) Nhu Y Shop (7) Long Mỹ Shop (8) Âu Hoa Leather Shop (9) Minh Thái Shop (10) Chung Bích Shop (11) Hảo Anh 1 Shop (12) Hảo Anh 2	IDST found 211 handbags, 156 wallets, 39 belts, 11 telephone boxes, 18 key hooks, 02 machine containers and 01 suitcase bearing infringed trademarks "LOUIS VUITTON", "LV", "Figure", "LV& Figure".	Foreign /Large	Domestic /Small	11-6-2009 /30-9-2009 /111	Administration	17,841	49	2,746	Confiscated and destroyed
PhuDong>< **PhuDongThienVuong** Registration No.32102	Two restaurants: one's name is "Phu Dong" and the other is "Phu Dong Thien Vuong". Their owners used to the co-founders of "Phu Dong". The two trademarks "PhuDong" & "PhuDongThienVuong" were registered and granted at NOIP for protection. PhuDong sued PhuDo		Domestic /Small	20-12-1999 /26-2-2003 /1,164	Civil court	15,510	50	3	Withdrew license

APPENDIX 8. Copyrights' Infringement

Case	Description	IP Owner /Size	IP Infringer /Size	Start date /End date /Duration (days)	Types of settlement	USD/ VND	Fine Millions VND	Fine USD	Extra penalty
Elsevier>< Vietnamese Individual	Elsevier found someone from Vietnam offered to sell books and articles of Elsevier over the internet without Elsevier authorization. Elsevier asked D&N (IP law firm) to represent Elsevier to solve the matter. D&N contacted Chief inspector of Ministry of Information and Communication.	Foreign /Large	Domestic /Small	1-6-2008 /1-8-2008 /61	Administration	16,790	123	7,326	Removed the infringed website
Vietnam Centre of Protection Music Copyright (VCPMC)>< TruyenThongPI	Inspectorates Department of Ministry of Culture, Tourism and Sport (IDCTS) found TruyenThongPI infringed the copyrights by broadcasting Music online without permission of authors.	Domestic /Small	Domestic /Small	8-4-2010 /7-5-2010 /29	Administration	19,030	20	1,051	
American Embassy>< FPT Telecom	American sent an official notification to Ministry of Foreign Affairs to complain about the copyright infringement of FPT Telecom, which had been publishing TV programs over the internet without permission. IDCTS found FPT Telecom infringed the copyrights of those TV programs.	Foreign /Large	Domestic /Medium	25-8-2008 /23-10-2008 /60	Administration	16,850	20	1,187	

The Internetional Federation of the Phonographic Industry: (IFPI)><Vi Na	IFPI requested IDCTS to investigate the copyright infringement of Vi Na for broadcasting music online without asking for permission of authors. IDCTS found that Vi Na had infringed the copyright.	Foreign /Large	Domestic /Small	1-3-2010 /11-5-2010	/72Administration	19,060	30	1,574